LIKE A TREE PLANTED

The Life Story
of

LESLIE RAY MARSTON

by

George L. Ford

With excerpts from
the writings, addresses,
and journals of L. R. Marston

Light and Life Press
Winona Lake, Indiana 46590

Library of Congress Catalog Card Number: 85-61115

ISBN: 0-89367-109-6

Printed in the United States of America
by Light and Life Press
Winona Lake, Indiana 46590

LESLIE RAY MARSTON
1894-1979

PSALM 1

Blessed is the man that walketh not in the counsel of the ungodly, nor standeth in the way of sinners, nor sitteth in the seat of the scornful.

But his delight is in the law of the Lord; and in his law doth he meditate day and night.

And he shall be like a tree planted by the rivers of water, that bringeth forth his fruit in his season; his leaf also shall not wither; and whatsoever he doeth shall prosper. . . .

For the Lord knoweth the way of the righteous. . . .

Acknowledgments

How do you tell the story of a great man you have known and respected? How do you keep your regard for him from clouding your objectivity? How do you let both his greatness and his humanness show?

Fortunately, Leslie Ray Marston helped us answer these questions. He left journals, books, and correspondence for us to follow.

My wife Esther worked side by side with me throughout the entire project. We spent three days at Greenville College reading the correspondence and reports he wrote while there. At the Free Methodist Church Headquarters in Winona Lake, Indiana, we went through the files for the twenty-nine years he served as bishop.

The National Academy of Science, which took over the work of the National Research Council, furnished background material. The Rockefeller Archive Center shared records of the support of NRC by the Laura Spellman Rockefeller Memorial. The National Association of Evangelicals furnished information from its publications and records. Asbury Theological Seminary provided material relating to Dr. Marston's service on its board.

Most of all, we thank Mrs. Evelyn Mottweiler, Dr. Marston's daughter and Executive Secretary of the Marston Memorial Historical Center in Winona Lake, Indiana. She gave us invaluable assistance by furnishing material and reading the manuscript.

—G.L.F.

Further acknowledgment and appreciation is given to John and Mary Benson who did extensive editorial work and book design, and saw the project through the press to completion.

—E.L.M.

Contents

(continued on next page)

Foreword

This is the story of Leslie Ray Marston, a "bashful boy" who excelled in scholarship, scientific research, and leadership. Seeing how he overcame his reticence can help anyone who shares his temperament, and those with more outgoing personalities will find in his life valuable lessons in leadership.

Leslie Marston had the usual characteristics of the introvert—reserve, the tendency to inaction, perfectionism, and self-depreciation. These traits stayed with him throughout his life. He needed positive reinforcement. How then did he rise to positions of recognition in fields as varied as research, child development, higher education, and church leadership?

To begin with, he had high intelligence. His academic achievements showed ability to grapple with tough problems and find answers. He did not limit himself to a narrow bank of academic pursuits, but scored high on a broad-based curriculum and branched out further in independent study. When he applied his mind to his multi-career work, he found answers and inspired others to follow him.

Also, because of his industry, Marston got more done than most people. He worked hard. As we studied his journals, read his letters, and combed through materials from his four major professions, we marveled at the intensity of his work. Perhaps this came in part from his fear of failure and his innate perfectionism. He never underprepared, and some thought he overprepared.

Finally, we must consider the word that best describes him: integrity. He always stood for the truth and what he thought was right. He became known for his tenacity, and some thought it was a fault. But it was tenacity for the right as he saw it.

We hope you see the real Leslie Marston in this book. If you do, his life may make your life better.

George L. Ford

Introduction

The biography of Leslie Ray Marston is a command performance. His significant contribution to his denomination and the larger evangelical community makes it necessary.

This scholarly administrator gave twenty-nine of his most productive years to the general superintendency of his church. No Christian leader has made a greater impact upon the character and mission of the Free Methodist Church since Benjamin Titus Roberts, its founder, in 1860.

Born in Michigan in a log house, the son of a preacher who ministered in both Wesleyan and Free Methodist churches, Leslie Marston never cut away from his roots. Converted in his youth, but with no clear call to the ministry, he nevertheless chose the way of service even in his secular profession. He became a child psychologist with a doctorate from the University of Iowa.

Within five years of the completion of his doctorate, Dr. Marston's brilliant scholarship brought him to national attention. Before he was thirty, he was appointed executive secretary of the National Research Council's Committees on Child Development, with offices in Washington, D.C. In 1930, he participated in the White House Conference on Child Health and Protection.

The church called Leslie Marston into the ministry. His first call came from his alma mater, Greenville College, in Illinois. His commitment to Christian service led him to accept the call. He surrendered his nationally prominent position. To the consternation of some of his peers among scholars, he gave up his scientific research. It was a radical change in the course of his career, seemingly a costly one from the world's viewpoint. He was thirty-three years old when he became president of Greenville College. From then to the end of his life he served his church as he served his Lord.

Dr. Marston was never the pastor of a local congregation. But friends urged him to accept ordination from his denomination while still president of Greenville. Again he took to heart the summons of the church as being God's guidance in life. He was ordained. In this manner God prepared this scientist-educator for the bishopric to which he was elected in 1935.

As a bishop, Dr. Marston became a pastor to the entire church. His congregation extended around the world and his pastoral care will be remembered for many years.

Marston's leadership was accepted in evangelical associations far wider than his church. He was a member of the executive committee of the World Methodist Council. He was among the founders of the National Association of Evangelicals and was its president from 1944 to 1946.

His spiritual authority in the leadership roles was eloquently testified to by Dr. Rufus Jones, of the Conservative Baptist Association, on an occasion when Jones was introducing him to a large audience of church leaders. "I have never heard Bishop Marston expound the doctrine of entire sanctification to which he and his church are committed," Jones said. "But I have watched him live it in the years we have served together on the Board of Administration of NAE."

All who knew this eminently talented and deeply devoted man will be grateful to have at hand the written record of his life. In the future, young people from our homes must have the privilege of knowing about Bishop Marston. They will find in his life what many of us have found—a role model for excellence in Christian character and service. We saw in him the incarnation of the spirit and mind that was in Christ.

Readers of this biography will be introduced to a great intellect and spirit. His gifts were many and awesome. He was an administrator, a teacher, a writer, a speaker, and a counselor. In all he excelled. His leadership reached everywhere Free Methodism has established churches. He used his talents to bring benefit to many interdenominational programs. His most profound offering, however, was his calm, reflective, wholesome devotion to Jesus Christ which marked all he did. He was a "Christ's man."

In this life story, the reader will see clearly those elements that create, as one has said, ". . . that mystery that finds explanation only in Jesus Christ," the truest witness that can be given. The direction of Marston's career choices, as well as his total investment of time and talent to the work God gave him to do, all point to the "mystery" in his responses to the demands and duties of Christian discipleship. His life was indeed "a living witness."

A book of his sermons has been published posthumously, titled, *He Lived on Our Street.* Bishop Marston was speaking of Jesus, of course, our incarnate God. But the bishop, too, lived on our street. He walked humbly with his God. His human and holy discipleship should add high octane fuel to the fires of renewal being kindled in the church today.

It seems appropriate that the Marston Memorial Historical Center, to which he gave his daily toil and gifted talents during retirement years, should have the privilege of publishing this fine biography of a great servant.

Paul N. Ellis
Chairman, Free Methodist
Historical Committee, and
Bishop Emeritus
of the Free Methodist Church

1

The Bashful Kid
From Michigan

The train sped through the late spring beauty of eastern Pennsylvania. With New York and Philadelphia behind, it rushed toward Harrisburg. There the huge electric engine would give way to a ponderous locomotive which with its superheated steam power would conquer the Appalachian Mountains as well as the miles that lay beyond.

A year later the train would carry a magic name: "The Spirit of St. Louis." But already it was the best way to travel. For one passenger this had special meaning. He sat at a desk in the last car writing a letter:

> Pennsylvania Railroad
> The St. Louisan
> The New Yorker

7:40 P.M.

Tues. June 1, 1926

Dear Parents:

I'm somewhere in Pennsylvania on one of the world's finest trains, the St. Louisan. It runs from New York to St. Louis in twenty-five hours, passing through Greenville, but not stopping. . . .

There are no coaches on this train, only sleepers, the diner, the club car, and the observation car. I am in the last named now at a fine writing desk. Easy chairs in the room, a library table with the latest magazines, etc. The track is quadruple to permit fast and slow traffic both ways without switching. I left New York at 4:50 today, and will be home at 4:29 tomorrow. We have been running three hours and have made, I believe, but one stop—at North Philadelphia. It costs extra to ride on this train—even above Pullman fare.

On these long trips, I have time to think about some things—have been thinking about you folks this evening in particular. Doesn't it seem strange that I should be where I am? I'm not in the least inclined to boast, but it is quite a step from being a green, bashful kid from the wilds of Michigan to a man with a national job, staying in high priced hotels, riding special fare trains, and associating with world-known scientists. This has come about without political or personal pull, but by the ability inherited from my parents and the advantages they have given me. . . . I'll never forget how Father encouraged me to "stay with it" at La Porte when I entered late from a poor school and became sorely discouraged, or how Mother's decisions against odds held steady.

Marriage has made quite a change in my personality. I am less retiring and more confident and assertive. Lila's very caution has strengthened me, for I have ventured out, assuming full responsibility for the outcome. I would probably have been ruined by another who would have made my decisions for me, and upon whom I would too largely depend.

I don't mean now that I have no temptations to discouragement. I have, and there are grave problems ahead. My hope is in good religion—so pray for me. This move I'm venturing is for a big purpose in the Kingdom, but there are hazards.

I'm not given to saying such things often, so when I do I mean them the more. Whatever I achieve, I'll have a deep feeling of gratitude to my parents, and I consider their investment in me a sacred trust which I hope never to fail.

With love,
Leslie

P.S. I expect that my travels sometime this year will lead me across Michigan.

Leslie Marston came, as he described it, from "the wilds of Michigan," but back of that lay a rich heritage. His father, John

Richardson Marston, is thought to have descended from the Marstons of England. The family name came from William the Conqueror, who crossed to England from Normandy in 1066. To reward the commander of his forces, William bestowed upon him the title, "Marston" (Warrior). With the title went large estates in Yorkshire County, including Marston Moor. Centuries later this became the site of a decisive battle between Charles I and Cromwell in 1844. Cromwell's victorious forces were led by a General Leslie. (That could have been the source of Leslie Marston's name, but he did not claim the connection.)

In 1634, three Marston brothers, William, Robert, and John, came to America. They settled in Massachusetts, but a change in boundary put some of them in New Hampshire. Their family lines clearly trace into the nineteenth century.

Leslie's grandfather, Stephen P. Marston, was born in New Hampshire on May 22, 1814. (According to family tradition, Stephen's grandmother was an American Indian.) Stephen married a girl named Emeline and moved to Michigan.

John, Leslie's father, was born in Lapeer County, Michigan, on July 21, 1862. In his early manhood he attended Spring Arbor Seminary near Jackson to prepare for the ministry. The seminary did not limit its curriculum to ministerial studies, but also offered elementary and secondary work. So it was that John met Lucy Sanderson, a secondary student.

Lucy's mother was Edna Case, a direct descendant of a brother of Noah Webster. On December 13, 1863, she married Charles Sanderson, a cattle drover who lived near Albion, New York. Lucy was born there on October 6, 1867. The family moved to Sherwood, Michigan, where Lucy's mother attended a Free Methodist church. Lucy's mother was converted through the ministry of the church, but her father would have nothing to do with it. He opposed his wife's religious interests.

Lucy taught district school in her teens, and then went to Spring Arbor for her high school work. When her father learned of her interest in John Marston, he objected to their marriage. On July 26, 1884, the young couple eloped when Lucy was seventeen and John twenty-two. Her father said he would shoot John. But after the elopement they returned to her home. While John unhitched the horses, he kept his eye on his new father-in-law. At least by his silence, the older man accepted John as Lucy's husband.

After his graduation from seminary, John pastored several Free Methodist churches, interspersed with farming. One of his achievements was the high quality of his family. However, much of the credit for that must go to Lucy. She was a strong leader; he a good man who loved his wife and children.

To the young pastor, John Marston, and his wife Lucy (Sanderson), Leslie Ray was born in a log house in Maple Ridge, Bay County, Michigan, on September 24, 1894, the last of seven children. A brother and two sisters died in infancy, leaving two brothers, Edd and Charles, and one sister, Jennie.

When Leslie was two weeks old the family moved to Blanchard where his father then pastored a Wesleyan Methodist church. By the time he was three years old they rented a farm. Years later, Leslie described their life in his journal:

> The house was an unpainted four-room cottage with a summer kitchen, situated on a knoll surrounded on two sides by swamps and ponds. Across the road, hilly, wooded pasture lands led off to nowhere. Neighbors lived in three directions about a quarter of a mile distant. My parents were industrious and soon were able to annex the adjoining "forty," the house from which was added to our earlier house, increasing the size but adding none to the architectural beauty of the dwelling.
>
> Just as I was turning five, I began to attend school regularly, a half-mile away. . . . The school was surrounded on three sides by woods—largely tamarac and evergreens—and rather swampy. In these woods we gathered wintergreens, adder's-tongues, lady's-slippers, jack-in-the-pulpits, and other flowers. Here also we built huts. The school grounds were sufficiently large for the traditional games in which I engaged with pleasure.
>
> In those days the teachers in rural schools were contracted by the term, three months. Thus there was a succession of teachers, good, bad, and indifferent. Some of them boarded at our house. I had but one man teacher in my first six years of school, and he was a poor one, in spite of the fact that my father was one of the directors of the school.
>
> The community was not very religious. Sunday school and sometimes preaching services were held at the school by the Wesleyans. Most parents in the community took little interest

in these religious activities.

My parents during this period returned to the Free Methodist Church to which both belonged by training and earlier membership. They drove several miles to church, usually leaving the children at home to attend services at the schoolhouse—an unprofitable if not positively injurious arrangement for the children. As a child of six and seven years I spent long Sunday afternoons in the company of older boys whose conversations and conduct were far from commendable. The moral tone of the community was lax.

Life during those years for the Marstons was frugal, simple, but not severe. We never knew want, but luxuries were quite unknown.

Memories of the five or six years of this period:

The spring on the hillside from which we carried water for household use, walled with stones and housed, with a pole across the center to which we held while dipping up the water. How refreshing the memory of the spring, and the drinks from the coconut-shell dipper! One day, alas! I slipped and fell into the spring. That evening Father cleaned out the spring.

The woods. The orchard. The hills and wilds to the westward where we gathered blackberries. The swimming hole. The roadside, where I, alone or with my sister, herded the cows.

A visit to my grandparents in southern Michigan, by horses and carriage one hundred and twenty miles, just Mother and the four children. . . .

Punishment administered by my mother, following which I enjoyed with her the finest fellowship of my young life. . . .

One day, when my father, with whom I was alone at home, took me in his arms with uncontrollable emotion— grief from some cause unknown to me.

As childhood advanced to boyhood and youth, I came to recognize that although Father provided us with basic principles of conduct, it was Mother who effectively applied them. I can recall no single occasion when Father laid hands on me in punishment—he didn't need to. Mother was equal to that task.

Early religious exercises of Free Methodist informality in that area were somewhat disturbing to my sensibilities, and the family was much amused once when, at perhaps four years of age, I complained that the meetings . . . "made me nervous."

I can recall the uneasiness when, still young, I returned home from school in the afternoon to hear from inside the house . . . prayer incident to a pastoral call on my parents.

Clearly etched in memory is the dreadful awe that came over me at a communion service . . . when the solemnity of the occasion led me to plead with my mother not to leave me in the pew alone while she met with the other adults at the communion rail according to Methodist custom. To this day I have warm appreciation for my mother's compliance with her disturbed child's request. (At that time children were not expected to present themselves for sacred communion with their parents.) . . .

Because of our frontier circumstances, the marks of history were little in evidence. Everything was new. Perhaps those early limitations account for my avid interest in antiquity. An "old" abandoned logging road in the "slashings," overgrown with grass, the pine corduroy logs providing the roadbed, moss-covered, would give me the thrill of discovery— although it may have been abandoned to nature only a decade or two earlier. No wonder that in my adult world travels, antiquity thrilled me to the core of my being.

My first "magic lantern" display of still pictures was in this period—shortly after the turn of the century, and as well, the first automobile I ever saw—probably a Stanley or White Steamer. My first auto ride, a high-wheeler with steel rimming its wheels, was around 1906. I was . . . twelve years or older before I talked on a telephone or encountered a flush toilet. . . .

After five years in the rather remote area of Mecosta County, Michigan, I changed to the Ensley Center School for my sixth grade because Father, after a period of location* following two pastorates with the Wesleyan Methodists . . . resumed his ministry with the Free Methodists, and was appointed to the Ensley circuit.**

---

*Location: a term used for pastors not actually serving churches.
**Circuit: usually two or more churches served by one pastor.

Along in June of our year at Ensley, the district camp meeting was held in a grove near Lakeview. Children's meetings were a feature of the program, and it was in one of these services that my sister and I were moved by the Holy Spirit to seek forgiveness, and we found peace with God. I was ten years of age, and Jennie was thirteen. Both of us received a very definite and glorious assurance of God's pardoning favor. Through all succeeding years—in college and university, the army, my professional life in the world, and forty-five years in Christian service, there has been no doubt about [my being saved, or] the validity of that event as a work of divine grace. . . .

The following account of Leslie's experience of entire sanctification is excerpted from an article he wrote for publication years after the event:

. . . I asked my preacher-father about entire sanctification when about twelve years of age; and later in my father's church I sought the experience, but afterward came to realize that the deliverance which came to me then was deliverance from a measure of backsliding. I soon discontinued the profession of entire sanctification.

When fourteen, in a camp meeting, again I sought the experience of entire sanctification, and in the midst of my seeking there came to me a relief and a blessing so similar to the earlier experience that I knew it was but the clearing of the rubbish in preparation for my seeking God's cleansing of my nature. Accordingly, I resumed prayer without leaving the altar, and came through to remarkable deliverance from the principle of sin with an overwhelming sense of cleanness. . . .

I mention an incident in my seeking which demonstrates how altar-workers may try to do the work of the Holy Spirit by suggesting details of surrender which the Spirit does not prompt. In the midst of my earnest pleading, a mature worker urged, "Yes, Lord! I'll give up baseball." Remember, I was fourteen years old. And I fairly lived baseball of the vacant-lot, scrub variety. My pleading moderated as I pondered this surrender. I was perplexed and confused. Finally I committed the problem to God, postponing decision until He should make the matter plain, but declaring my willingness to do His will. And victory came, with no decision concerning baseball but with an unqualified decision to obey God. The next day I sought out my adviser and asked him to explain his counsel that I give up baseball. "Oh," he said, "I meant Sunday baseball!" But Sunday baseball had never even tempted me, and his running ahead of the Spirit all but blocked my reaching the victory of a clean heart.

Following my breaking through to full victory, a struggle of faith again drove me to the secret place that I might maintain this new relationship to God in full surrender and constant cleansing. After a prolonged period of struggle, during which my father joined in my prayer battles and gave mature counsel, I came through to a more established experience. . . .

Soon Father was appointed to Sunfield circuit for two years, and I had my first contact with a village school of more than one room and teacher. In this school I completed grades seven and eight. . . .

Early in our residence in Sunfield occurred an experience with a bully of the community. He lived in "the mansion on the hill." His father was the hardware merchant in whose store I had purchased my first commercially mounted kite. I was in a field back of the church sheds where the horses were kept. I was playing with the wonderful new kite when the village bully saw me and moved in to take the kite—or perhaps destroy it. I grappled with him and threw him down in the dirt of the field and held him there until a friendly teenager of our own church community came to my help. I dared let the bully get to his feet, his viciousness somewhat subdued.

Relating the day's incident in the family circle that evening, I felt quite saintly for the restraint I had exercised in not pummeling the bully. Mother asked why I didn't give him a good thrashing. I have an idea she knew I needed such advice. . . .

Leslie did well in school, as his eighth grade (1908) report card shows. (See page 24).

His success in school deserves special recognition in light of the frequent moves of the family. Pastors did not serve long in one place at that time. The times of "location" added to the unsettled life.

Leslie continued his story in his journal:

> Father's next appointment was to Lakeview, a larger vil-
> lage and a larger school. Before the school year closed, my
> parents moved to a farm, again near Blanchard and about a
> mile from our former home in this area. But I boarded in
> Lakeview, about twelve miles from the new family residence,
> and completed my first year in Lakeview High School.
>
> The following year I attended the Blanchard High School,
> a two-year institution, a type later known as a junior high
> school. . . . This year at Blanchard I lost time because the
> curricular offerings were limited for one who had pursued a
> regular course in a larger school. Here I gained some notori-
> ety for my crude pictorial efforts, one such portraying Princi-
> pal Jarred punishing a student—a picture that came to the
> principal's attention and seemed to amuse him. Our farm
> home, which we called "Fairview," was about three and
> one-half miles from the school, and I walked that distance in
> good weather. I finished this junior high school in 1909.
>
> My father's oldest brother was at that time district elder
> [now called superintendent] in the old North Indiana Confer-
> ence of the Free Methodist Church, and he desired Father to
> serve with him—which Father did for two years while leaving
> his membership in the North Michigan Conference. He was
> appointed to the Springville and La Porte circuit, but as
> conference was held in the fall and I was late arriving, the La
> Porte High School already had been in session a matter of
> weeks.
>
> This was my first city school—and it was a good one. I
> was handicapped because of my year at Blanchard, lacking
> acceptable units to qualify me as a full junior. I adjusted to
> the problem and spent three more years in high school, two
> of them at La Porte. Here I had my first opportunity for
> training in art. For a time I had thought of being a cartoonist,
> but perhaps it was the formal training that cooled my en-
> thusiasm and weakened my confidence in my talent. As the
> years passed, I sought to satisfy my urge in the pictorial field
> by making amateur photography a hobby.
>
> While in La Porte, I competed in public speaking, won the
> local declamatory contest, and went to South Bend for the
> district meet, where I placed fifth, about midpoint of those

competing. My declamation was Patrick Henry's "Give Me Liberty, or Give Me Death!"

The Springville point was the central charge of the circuit, and the location of the parsonage, five and one-half miles from La Porte. But now I was the possessor of a bicycle which I rode both ways daily, except during the winter period. Springville was a delightful woodsy hamlet, and it was here I began using the church for my early sermonic attempts. While practicing my declamation for the contest, I sometimes resorted to the woods, and the trees were my audience. This was the occasion of some merriment in the hamlet, for Joe, living at the foot of the Springville hill, was given on occasion to drink, and then would express the "spirits" he had imbibed by preaching. The neighbors, hearing my voice in declamation breaking out of the woods, wondered if Joe had been drinking again!

At the close of my second year in La Porte High, I found my first factory job at Dumley Oil-Drill as a painter. The wage was good for those days—$2.00 for a ten-hour day. After a time the paint boss proposed taking me off straight painting and making me a striper or decorator. In honesty, I told him I would be leaving for school at summer's close.

But the job was a part of my education. I came to better understand the laboring man, and the problems of the honest worker, for my companion painters opposed my diligence in doing the job I was paid to perform.

The summer of 1911, Father returned to the North Michigan Conference.

. . . He was assigned to County Line Church about six miles northwest of Coopersville, where stood one of the oldest churches in the conference. . . . That year I attended the Coopersville High School and was graduated in 1912.

Rev. John Marston, Leslie's father, gave the invocation at graduation. Leslie delivered an oration, "Woman's True Relation to the World." So began his influence as an agent of change.

(Above) The Marston family in 1895. From left, Edd, John, Charles with Jennie in front, Lucy with Leslie Ray on her lap.

Jennie and Leslie in their school years.

Leslie's report card—8th grade—1908

PRIMARY OR GRAMMAR SCHOOL.			Sept.	Oct.	Nov.	Dec.	Jan.	Feb.	Mar.	April	May	June	Y'rly Av.
		Reading						95	100	100	100	50	99
		Spelling	93	99	98	98	93	90	100	98	78	49	96
		Writing	90	86	91	95	94	95	97	97	98		93
		Arithmetic ..	98	97	97	98	95	93	98	92	99	49	96
EXAMINATIONS.	examination has been held, the average of the recitations is given.	Geography ..											
		Grammar ...	93	98	97	100	97	*Final*					
		Language ...											
		Physiology ..					*Mich. Hist.*			97	50	96
		U.S. History .	96	93	96	84	95	92	99	94	*Final*		
		Civil Gov't ..	97	95	98	98	97	92	99	95 *State*	100	50	97
		Music	*Final*										
		Drawing ...											

In June 1912, Leslie graduated from high school in Coopersville, Michigan.

Leslie's natural ability to draw cartoons came out on many occasions.

SIMPLE SIMON
by LRM 1908

2

Agonies and Ecstasies
of Further Schooling

The summer of 1912 was wet and cold. The farm where Leslie worked to earn money for college had cold springs in its field. He got a dollar a day plus "keep," just half the money he received working in a factory the year before. All of this added up to a bad experience. But he confessed that his "incompetence and lack of fondness for the work" were his chief problems.

In spite of the problems, he worked through the summer, and when he arrived at Greenville College in southern Illinois in September, he continued working part time. He told of this period in later writings:

> Somewhere in my papers a few years ago I came across a small pocket notebook in which I had recorded my early college expenditures, one of the first items being "overalls." Having arrived a few days prior to opening, I went to work cleaning up the campus, earning thereby ten cents an hour. Campus wages and wages in general then were low. A year earlier I had earned twenty cents an hour as a factory worker, and thought I was well paid. But living expenses were also moderate at the college. As I recall, the college rate was about $3.75 per week for board and room at that time, and college tuition $60.00 a semester.
>
> Other means of college aid I resorted to included doing yard work in the neighborhood, waiting tables in the college

dining room (one of the choice jobs of the campus), acting
as an agent for the local laundry (detachable starched collars
then being the college [male] mode), selling flowers among
students for Mother's Day, and one year, teaching a class in
German in the preparatory school connected with the college.

One summer I joined the ranks of the brush salesmen, and
my territory was Belding, Michigan, a silk mill town where
my sister, Jennie, was then employed. I did very well with
the fresh, first-class kit of brush samples with which I started
out, but as my orders came back for delivery, I was dis-
tressed to find that the bristles of some of the items I was to
deliver were yellowed and definitely inferior to the imported
Chinese bristles of the samples from which I had made my
sales. I wrote my complaint to the firm and received an admission that, due to the World War [I], Chinese bristles could
not be imported and native bristles had been used. I was advised to work into my sample case the inferior items and sell
from them as samples. But I had lost heart . . . and turned to
other activities for the remainder of the summer.

With all his work Leslie did not neglect his studies or other activities. He took three years of German, two years of French, and
two years of mathematics. This with literature, economics, psychology, political science, ethics, chemistry, logic, philosophy, education, sociology, missions, oratory, and his honors thesis on
theism made a four-year college course that few could handle
well. But for Leslie it posed no problem. For the four years his
lowest grade was 90 percent; the highest 99. He averaged 94.8
percent.

The 1913 *Vista,* the college yearbook, carried a description of
Leslie written by his classmate and friend, Wilson R. King:

"Serious and responsible. Worthy of honor. Liable to over-
study. An orator with a fine voice. A good ball player in spite of
his ministerial air. Successful tennis manager."

Leslie graduated in June of 1916, magna cum laude, with a
good balance of work, sports, studies, and student activities. The
Vista listed his record:

Class treasurer 1913-1914
Student Organization President 1915-1916

Vista Organization Editor 1914-1915, Art Editor 1915-1916
Las Cortes Charter Member (Debate Club)
Phoenix President 1913 (Literary Club)
Consul 1914-1916
College Missionary Society Treasurer 1915-1916
Ministerial Association President 1913, Secretary 1915
Prohi Club President 1914-1915 (Speech Club)
Second Place Seaman Oratorical 1915
Class Baseball 1913-1914
Assistant Teacher Preparatory Department
Honors in Philosophy*

Begins Graduate Study

A University of Illinois scholarship opened the door for his graduate study, providing for his academic costs and a one-year stipend of $250 to help with his living expenses. His parents supplemented his funds so he could give full time to work on his master's degree.

Leslie tackled his graduate work with the same enthusiasm that had carried him through Greenville College. The load was heavy, as he explained:

At that date, Greenville was not fully accredited by the University, and the University imposed upon Greenville graduates an undergraduate handicap of from eight to sixteen hours. This meant that at least a quarter of a year's undergraduate credit must be completed, in addition to a full graduate year for the master's degree.

My undergraduate majors had been modern languages and a philosophy/education combination. As my master's field, I chose education as a major, philosophy as a minor. My undergraduate handicap I worked off in history and education.

At that period, the School of Education of the University of Illinois rated high—rivaling the University of Chicago and Columbia., At the top in the latter institution, if not of the nation, was John Dewey, pragmatic philosopher who was the apostle of "interest" in the education process—

---

*Department honors in philosophy were granted for his thesis, "Mysticism's Message to Our Age."

"experience centered." The Dean of Education at Illinois was William Chandler Bagley, the doughty apostle of "duty" who so clearly foresaw the ultimate consequence of the "soft pedagogy" of John Dewey in weakening the fibre of American Democracy. My work under Bagley was influential in shaping my direction in the area of learning and discipline.

The influence of Dr. Bagley on Leslie shows in the Seventeenth Yearbook of the National Society for the Study of Education. The yearbook included a paper by Leslie, H. S. McKown, apparently another graduate student, and Dr. Bagley. The paper discussed the misplacement of emphasis in seventh and eighth grade history textbooks for the years between 1765 and 1865. The writers found some misplacements of emphasis by the textbooks and suggested corrections. Leslie exhibited the same meticulous research methods and careful writing throughout his life. The recollections from his journal continued:

> My principal professor was a Dr. Johnston. With him, I developed my master's thesis on "The Place of Emotional Response in Literature," using as laboratory the Urbana City High School—an institution of high grade.
>
> My minor in philosophy was completed in a year-long seminar on English Ethics under Dr. Daniels, the only other member of the seminar being a Dr. Bentley of Stanford University, whose brother was head of the Illinois Department of Psychology. I was not the star member of this two-member seminar! I was in beyond my depth, but when my toes touched bottom I would push desperately to the surface to gasp and gulp a bit of air before sinking again out of sight! But Dr. Daniels, later Dean of the Graduate School, found some basis for passing me as "Satisfactory"!
>
> During the year 1916-1917, I completed all of the requirements—an eight-hour undergraduate differential, full course work, thesis, and final oral examination—and was then granted a graduate fellowship for the ensuing year on a higher stipend than the scholarship had afforded. It likewise demanded no services, but was to leave my time entirely free for study toward the doctorate. . . .

The grading system at the University used *E* (excellent) as the top grade and *S* (satisfactory) as second. Leslie received seven *E's* and four *S's* for the year.

During his year at the University, Leslie faced problems concerning his faith. They began near the close of his time at Greenville College, but the influence of Christian teachers there had strengthened him. Now, without the help of such men, the problems increased.

In the spring of his graduate year, a district rally of his church was held at Danville, Illinois, about thirty miles from the University. Professor John LaDue, affectionately known as "Rabbi" on the Greenville campus, was the guest speaker. Leslie went to the meeting. While there he asked LaDue to stop over for a day with him at the University. Dr. LaDue consented.

> That Monday night, and into Tuesday's morning hours, we discussed my problems, It was late when I went to a bed in the attic dormitory where the other men of the house were accustomed to sleep, leaving my bed for my guest.
>
> In our prolonged interview, at one point Professor LaDue said, "Marston, if there is a moral reason why you are perplexed in your faith, the outlook is dark. But if you desire to believe, I have little doubt of the outcome of your recent struggles."
>
> I knew that my desire was to believe, and the old professor's statement was to steady me in the months ahead— and to help lift me out of my perplexities of faith.

Some of the credit for Leslie's success in college, and especially at the University, must go to his parents. He always knew he had their moral support. And when he needed money, they came through.

> I would pay tribute to the help my parents provided in the matter of my schooling. . . . My parents knew how to "make do," and had managed on small earnings on "hard-scrabble circuits," and by farming in a modest way, to acquire a small estate. It was their philosophy that children should be helped to get started in life from family savings, rather than receive their portions of the family estate at the parents' death, after establishing themselves without parental help, or after failure without it. . . .

While in college and university, I helped myself as I was able without jeopardy to my studies, but knew that when I needed assistance with finances, my parents would find a way. This knowlege removed the pinch of distress over finances and enabled me to devote my energies to the task at hand.

Mother had inherited from her mother a jolly Irish streak which showed itself while I was in graduate school. My letter from home on one occasion enclosed a clipping:

Farmer Jones: "I hear as how your son is educated—has his B.A. and his M.A."

Farmer Brown: "That is so! Bill has his B.A. and his M.A., but his P.A. still supports him."

But my parents would not be guilty of partiality in favoring me. They balanced out their parental benefactions by giving my brothers . . . assistance in purchasing farms in the home neighborhood.

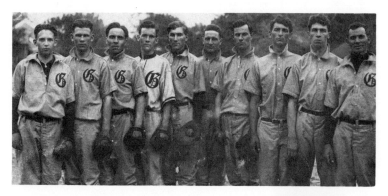

Greenville College baseball team, 1913-14, with Leslie fourth from left.

Leslie graduated from Greenville College, magna cum laude, in 1916. The University of Illinois gave him a scholarship to help with the cost of his first year of graduate study.

3

World War I Reaches
into Leslie's Life

The village of Lakeview, Michigan, turned out early on the morning of Saturday, March 30, 1918, to see the boys off. Words and tears flowed freely. Then the boys climbed into automobiles of some of the local citizens for the twenty-mile trip to Stanton, the county seat. Stanton received them enthusiastically and with the music of a band conducted them to the train.

Leslie Marston was in the army.

While many volunteered for service as soon as the United States entered the war,* most men were content to let the draft call them.

Leslie had chosen to wait until summoned. Having a fellowship for work on his doctorate, he had returned to the University of Illinois in the fall of 1917. But his graduate career was soon interrupted. In October he received notice from his draft board in Michigan to stand ready to report for military service on twenty-four hour notice. He wrote:

What was I to do in central Illinois and my residence in

*Many of the nations of Europe had been at war since the summer and fall of 1914. The United States assisted England, France, and other nations with money and supplies, but managed to stay out of the fighting for almost three years. Meanwhile, German submarines sank an increasing number of United States ships carrying munitions to the Allies. Because of this, the United States broke diplomatic relations with Germany on February 3, 1917. On April 6, Congress declared war with Germany. Before the end of the war, America would induct almost five million men into the armed services. Two million went to France and 115,000 died in combat and from other causes.

central Michigan? And if I remained in the University, how could I settle down to study with the possibility of a call to military service any day? I resigned my fellowship and returned home at once.

Back at the Marston home in Lakeview, he waited for several months because the military camps were not prepared to receive large groups of men. He did not fret over the delay, but took advantage of the time to settle some things in his mind, concerning which he noted:

> During those months, I did some careful thinking, and "found myself"—that is, clearly formulated my basic philosophy which, although it has further developed and grown clearer, has never since been shaken—during my approaching army experience, my further university studies, and my professional associations in the world.

So on that cold March morning, the troop train clattered through the villages and towns, while people gathered along the tracks to cheer them on. At Grand Rapids the Red Cross brought good lunches on board the train.

Leslie may have whistled in the dark when he started his first letter home that evening:

> Here I am sitting on my bunk and enjoying myself. I don't feel one bit lonesome or homesick and feel as though camp life will agree with me. . . .

Some of his other letters written to his home from Camp Custer were long and written over a period of several days. Some showed hope, encouragement, and expectations of advancement. Others expressed disappointment and frustration. He started one of the happier letters on April 4, 1918:

> I was very much pleased tonight just after "retreat" to hear . . . that I had some mail. . . . I experienced the happiest time of my brief army life perusing the contents of those letters. There was the letter from home and the pictures, the letters from the parsonage, and a letter from Jennie. Do it again.

I am feeling excellent tonight—especially since the mail has come. But say, never before do I recall desiring so much a chance at some of Mother's "eats." . . .

They are still feeding us in the open. As we finish, we form a line for two wash boilers of hot water. Perhaps seventy will be in line at one time. I very much dislike to be at the end of a long line. As our turn comes, we dip our mess kits into the first boiler, sozzle them around, perhaps lose our knife, spoon, and fork in its soapy depth and have to fish them out, then complete the cleansing (?) process in the second boiler. . . .

While I have been writing this, you have been in prayer meeting and have prayed for me. I wonder how many of these boys have prayers offered for them?

Four days later he again wrote home:

I wrote to Dr. Whipple of the University and received word today that I have been recommended to Major Yerkes, the psychologist, for work in psychology. . . . I hope I may be placed in some field of service in which I may use my previous training and receive additional training of a nature to help me in my line. . . .

Well, I've signed up for $10,000 of insurance, $5,000 to go to each of you. But would you feel badly if I would make a different disposition of a part of it? I know you have sacrificed for me, but if anything happens that I shouldn't be able to do anything in the world, I would like it if some of my insurance money could work for me. This insurance isn't paid up [paid back] all at once, but $57.50 per month for twenty years. Would you be willing to let $30.00 per month go, either to support a missionary or as a scholarship for the preparation of suitable candidates for missionary work? That would leave only $27.50 per month for you. I don't want you to feel that I'm ungrateful, but if you are not in need, I would like to have my insurance provide a substitute.

Leslie's concern for a substitute if he "shouldn't be able to do anything in the world" reveals a consistent character quality. His integrity was not limited to doing nothing evil. He wanted to do something good. The possibility of dying in the war didn't, in his mind, relieve him of that responsibility. This integrity would become one of the marks of his greatness.

By mid-April, he had high hopes of getting into psychology work with the Medical Department. Dr. Whipple's recommendation had reached the office of the Surgeon General of the United States Army. If accepted, he would spend two months training in military psychology at Ft. Oglethorpe, Georgia. In his enthusiasm he cautioned himself, "I must not build too high hopes."

He asked his folks to send him one of his books by Whipple and another psychology book. He started his homework and waited for the call that never came.

But the officers of the camp now knew his qualifications. Not many recruits had master's degrees. His university work in psychology fitted him for special jobs in the camp. Perhaps these things worked against his transfer to the work he wanted.

Late in April, he came down with the mumps. He told his parents about it:

> Here I am now at the Base Hospital. It is quite pleasant here. . . . They are keeping me in bed yet, however. . . . I sent a letter last night after I reached the hospital and was obliged to tear the corners of the envelope off so the letter could be fumigated. . . .
>
> I have viewed my face in the glass with considerable amusement. And could you have seen me, you would have laughed also. I reminded myself of a blow snake. It is my opinion that a full-faced person in at least one respect looks less odd with mumps than a long spare-faced creature like myself. . . .
>
> New patients arrive quite often, and those who have served their allotted time in pajamas and bathrobes are sent back to their barracks where they are deprived of both. Yes! we even have pillows and sheets here, and white coverlets on our beds, and we eat with table instruments of quite delicate proportions! And all the time our pay goes on the same as though we were drilling in the field or writing in an office. . . . And yet I have a harder time to keep from "knocking" here than in the barracks. The perversity of human nature. . . .
>
> There is another important article of our hospital equipment which I must mention—the mask—"gas mask," we call

it. It is a rectangular piece of cloth made of thick material. It is an offence punishable by court martial for a patient to leave his bed with his mask off. . . .

This place reminds me somewhat of a monastery, and its occupants with their bathrobes serving the purpose of gowns, and with their "gas masks" instead of cowls, are monks. . . .

When Leslie returned to his barracks two weeks later, he found most of his quarter mates gone. They had shipped out to Georgia en route to France. His sergeant told him he would leave Saturday, but he didn't. On Sunday he was free for the first time in camp. He went to the YMCA services morning and evening.

On Monday he was transferred to the Medical Department to work in the psychiatric ward of the Base Hospital. Though he wore the maroon and white hat cord of the Medical Department, this wasn't the job he applied for. It did not include the special training he wanted. He received no advance in rank; his pay remained at $30.00 a month. In fact, at this point he had not been paid. He worked twelve hours a day, seven days a week, with almost no opportunity to attend religious services. But he found some things he liked. Leslie especially appreciated the ward surgeon, Captain Odom, as he explained to his parents:

Everybody likes him, save perhaps some of his patients. Somehow he must have learned of my interest in psychology, for yesterday he opened the subject and then offered me some valuable opportunities. When I am occupied with nothing else, I have free access to one of his books, and when I have mastered that I hope to have use of others. He even said he would allow me to apply tests to the inmates. I can see how my work in the notorious Ward 33 may be of great value to me. I shall not concern myself much regarding Ft. Oglethorpe school. Later I may be able to get in there.

The opportunities for advancement here [Ward 33] are somewhat limited it would seem. Further, members of this detachment are not candidates for the officers' school, so that avenue of advancement is closed. But a few months' work accompanied by study may be worth more to me than advancement in another line, should that be possible. . . .

The pressure of his job soon began to tell on Leslie. On the evening of May 20, he continued a letter he had started that morning:

> When will I have time to finish this letter? Time is at a premium with me now. Up about 5:40. Then reveille at 6:00, calisthenics, breakfast and off to work by 7:00. Off duty at 7:00 tonight, but studied for a time and just reached home a short time ago. It is now 8:30. Lights are supposed to go out at 9:00. I shall shave after lights are out—to save time. The lights don't go out in the bathhouse. . . .
>
> Give $1.00 to the preacher toward that self-denial fund for missions. . . . Will settle at payday which I hope will be soon. . . .

As days and weeks wore on, both good and bad came his way. He watched beside the beds of would-be suicides. He encouraged men in despair. To a man who wondered if his mother would forgive him for the way he had treated her he said, "Of course, mothers always do."

Captain Odom supervised his giving psychometric tests and encouraged him.

> Last night I was in the office alone recording temperatures, etc., when the captain entered. . . . He said he thought it would be only a matter of time before I would get a commission, and I have the assurance of his assistance. But the army is an uncertain place, there's many a slip. For the present, I am satisfied to be here. Isn't it strange how we plan, and then our plans come to naught and a better way is opened?
>
> This morning Captain Odom asked me if I wanted to take a trip. One of the patients must be escorted to his home in Marquette County. I told the captain I was a Puritan in my attempts to observe the Sabbath, and rather than travel on that day, I preferred someone else should go. . . . He did a little calculating to see how soon the patient's red tape could be wound up. . . . Should the affairs go through and the papers come back before Sunday, I shall have to go—it is one of the necessities of war.

Leslie made two such necessary trips, the one to Marquette

County, and one to Newberry, Michigan. His pay finally came through on June 7. He received $36.80 for two months and two days after deductions for insurance and laundry. He told his folks, "I believe I'll make the last payment on the Greenville pledge, including Jennie's part. . . . Then I believe I'll send the pastor at Greenville about $2.50 to pay my claims (conference assessments) and have a little for himself. . . ."

A week later his discouragement began to show:

> I've been here a month now. Today I don't feel very well satisfied, but I may be in a passing mood of depression. This work is so confining, and I don't like some things about the organization. But the ward surgeon is fine. . . .
>
> Last night I and others were tested by a psychologist. The tests, some of them, were similar in nature to the ones given here, but cover a much greater range of difficulty. I wish I were giving those tests with a silver bar on my shoulder instead of in a white uniform. I am now a First Class Private and have the insignia on my sleeve. . . . My pay is increased by $3.00 per month!
>
> My church privileges are almost nil, and Sunday differs little from other days. Again I say, "Oh, the grind!"

> June 24, 1918
> I am thinking of applying soon to get into the school at Ft. Oglethorpe. I see more and more that I am deserving of some special recognition. Sounds big-headed, does it? . . .
>
> I am not feeling so badly as I did for a time. "What's the use of worrying," the soldiers often sing. In the past I have been greatly troubled before success. Is success ahead? I don't know. . . .

> July 1, 1918
> Your card received today. I'm feeling some better recently. . . .
>
> Captain Odom has been very good to me, but he has been transferred to another camp. His departure was quite sudden. . . . Before leaving he did me a good turn. He took time to supervise the writing of a letter to the Surgeon General at Washington concerning an assignment to psychological service for me, and attached to the letter his recom-

mendation. In fact, his recommendation is one of the things that bothers me—he gave me credit for familiarity with a psychometric test with which I am not any too familiar, but am making myself so as I can.

I have a request to make—please say nothing about it. If I'm disappointed, others don't need to know it. If I'm successful, then it will be a delightful surprise. Think of it—if only I could get into the psychological service. Drafted as a private, of course, and having done very menial work in the army, and then to get a commission would be quite a leap. Can I keep my head, should it happen? I guess so. But please don't mention my prospects to anyone. . . .

July 8, 1918

Whether or not I get a commission I am learning a lot here in the ward. Isn't it remarkable that I should be able to study along my line? Now if only I can get to Ft. Oglethorpe. Well, I've done my part, and if I don't hear from my application there is no need of fretting. . . .

July 12, 1918

Matters aren't running very satisfactorily at the ward. The new ward master is very lazy and a lot falls on the rest of us. It would be easy for me to have a row with him. How long will things continue as they are? I'm disappointed in not hearing from my application. . . .

Today a lieutenant from down in camp called me regarding psychological service. He said he would be up to the Base to a meeting tonight and would like to see me. We talked things over. I told him my qualifications, and he told me what the work down there in camp would be like. The hours are much shorter than here, and ordinarily, Saturday afternoons and Sundays off. . . . I'll not have anything great—no commission nor anything like it—but the work will be good, clean office work with respectable hours, and the opportunity to get off to church and to Jackson and possibly home.

July 27, 1918

Am transferred. Moved to other end of camp. . . . I have time now to read and visit. I'm feeling quite well. The grind

of the Base is gone. Of course, there are perplexities, etc.,
but on the whole I like it. . . .

Leslie soon became chief clerk in the Psychological Office. But a
foreboding entry in his diary introduced a new and devastating
enemy: "October—Influenza epidemic. Office closed. Nursed
nights in emergency ward. Virtually in charge."

It began at Camp Funston, Kansas, on March 11, 1918, and
spread rapidly to Camp Kearney in California and then to Ft. Oglethorpe, Georgia. The war kept the disease out of the headlines,
so it gained no general notice.

In May, Funston's divisions carried influenza to France where it
spread through both Allied and enemy forces. It soon became an
international epidemic.

By the time the influenza returned to America, it was pandemic.
Bodies lay unburied because graves could not be dug fast enough.
The disease prostrated whole families with no one to care for
them.

Most of the deaths came from secondary infections, especially
pneumonia. Worldwide deaths totaled twenty million. In America
500 thousand died, almost five times as many as were killed in the
war.

As his diary entry showed, Leslie was caught in the midst of
this. When the Psychological Office closed because of the epidemic, his hospital experience made him a natural to work in the
emergency ward and take leadership.

One hundred miles away in Alma, Michigan, Leslie's sister, Jennie, was completing her nurse's training at Brainerd Hospital. Their
letters tell their own stories in the midst of the plague:

September 14, 1918
Dear Brother:

I suppose you went to church today. I am going this evening if I can. Two months and one-half left for me. Guess
will come out about right with the book work. Saw operation
the other day that I have never seen before, and Dr. B. said
I would not likely see again.

November 3, 1918
Dear Brother:

I didn't write home so often as I should this week. So

Mother phoned last evening. Father is pretty old to have pneumonia and get along as well as he has.

I am well, but we've had plenty to do. The night nurse has the influenza. That left just two of us for day and night. So we worked hard all day, then one would stay on duty at night. Dr. Brainerd said to sleep between calls, but not much rest that way, then keep going all next day till night. . . .

Camp Custer, Michigan
October 8, 1918, 1:30 a.m.
Dear Sister:

If you look at the hour at which I am writing this, you may guess that I am on night duty. The epidemic has been raging here about ten days now. Last week Monday, fifty of our men, and I among them, were detailed to the Base Hospital on special duty to assist in the rush. . . .

I had worked in the office all day, and that evening at 7:00 I went on duty in one of the several improvised hospitals at our end of camp. . . . It's a strenuous life, but I'm standing up under the strain in fine shape. . . .

P.S. October 12, 1918, 12:15 a.m.

It has been some time since I started this letter, and I have received yours. I am still working nights, and I am getting pretty well fatigued. This morning while taking pulse rates, I would doze off and lose my count, or perhaps recover myself and wonder if I had missed my count or not. . . .

Today the two wards on this floor were combined under one surgeon. He placed me over both wards—or what were two wards. The man who has been in charge of the other ward is a druggist and knows much more about medicine than I. It is my opinion that he is rather "peeved" because I am in charge. . . .

Just when do you graduate? You should feel honored that Dr. Brainerd wants you to stay. . . .

On October 17, Leslie received a telegram from the Red Cross that said, "Your brother died this morning." Leslie obtained a pass to attend Charles' funeral. Charles had experienced forgiveness of sins on his deathbed and had given his parents clear confirmation of his peace with God.

Four weeks after Leslie returned to camp, his mother sent an ominous letter saying that Jennie had the flu. Three postcards from his mother quickly followed.

Postal Card. At depot. Going to Alma. Had dispatch from Dr. Brainerd. Jennie is worse. Pa will come. She wrote she was better. Train coming. Will let you know how she is. I called Dr. He said she was not seriously sick.

Postal Card. Monday evening, Alma Post Office:
Sent you card today telling Jennie was worse. Guess she was in quite critical condition last night—fever 105° and above and still rising. They put her in tub of cold water, then cold pack, did no good. She is better, fever 103° plus. Very, very weak. I don't know what to do about having Pa come down. He is so weak. They think Jennie is coming all right unless something sets in. No pneumonia. I cannot go back now. My, but we are having our share of trouble. Hope you keep well.

Postal Card. Dear boy: Will try to write a line and tell you how Jennie is. I can hardly tell you, but she has put in a dreadful night of suffering. She is far from being out of danger. I am worried about her. What seems so hard is not to be able to relieve her. I surely had lots to bear up under and seems so much has depended on me, Pa being so poorly and weak. . . . Oh, pray for us here, Leslie, it's so hard. Jennie's suffering is principally her back, no pneumonia. Temperature last night, 102° and now 102.7°. Take care of yourself. I couldn't stand any more. Will drop a line often; you will be anxious.
                    Mother.
Dr. just here (pneumonia). How will I phone you?

Jennie, Leslie's beloved sister, died the next morning, just eleven days before completing her nurse's training. Jennie's passing was one of glorious victory. She had been a Christian witness in her hospital service, and a hospital room was later named in her memory. Her diploma was issued posthumously to her parents.

Soon after Jennie's death, Leslie's army experience began to change. The influenza epidemic abated. With the Armistice on November 11, demobilization began. Ten days later he was transferred to the Medical Department of the 40th Infantry Division. On December 8, the division moved to Camp Sherman, Ohio. There he became Chief Clerk of the Regional Infirmary. His promotion to sergeant came on June 21, 1919. He received his discharge on July 31.

In the spring of 1917, the University of Illinois permitted graduating males to return to farms and shops to engage in the war effort during the several days between the completion of school work and graduation.

This picture presents the young Master of Arts, whose diploma had reached him by mail on his parents' Edgewood Farm near Lakeview, Michigan. He is fully dressed for the job with a hay fork in one hand and his Master's diploma in the other. (Caption by L.R.M.)

The young recruit in his quarters "devouring" a recent letter from home.

Leslie's love for children shows up in unexpected places, even in war time.

Official portrait of Leslie Marston in 1918 just before the influenza epidemic hit their camp (but missed him).

Much of his time was spent in office work—record-keeping, mail, with telephone interruptions providing occasional relief from the monotony.

Medical detachment of the 40th Infantry in full uniform. Leslie, front, third from right.

4

The Bachelor
Meets and Marries
Lila Lucile Thompson

After his release from the army, Leslie applied for the renewal of his fellowship at the University of Illinois. While he waited for an answer, he struggled with the fear that he might again face intellectual conflict. Perhaps he should accept a position offered him by Greenville College, one of the schools of his church and his alma mater. He could avoid the challenges to his faith that way. It was while wrestling with these thoughts on his mind that he visited his sister Jennie's grave. Looking back on this period, he wrote:

> At the graveside I longed to exchange places with her, lest returning to intellectual pursuits I might lose my faith. And from her graveside on a beautiful moonlit night, I walked alone into the country to fight my battle. Finally, it came to me forcibly that if I accepted the position then offered me . . . for fear of what might happen to me, I would be poorly qualified to help other youth with their problems of doubt and faith. On that basis I settled the matter, and thereafter, although subjected to the currents of unbelief in different relationships of life, my faith prevailed and inner conflict never again crippled me.

He received the fellowship and returned to the University of Illinois in September 1919. But he soon became disappointed with what he found. Most of the professors under whom he had studied were gone. Their replacements did not challenge him, except Dr. B. H. Bode. And the challenge was to his faith.

Leslie took work in the philosophy of education from Dr. Bode. Bode was a disciple of John Dewey, the noted educational pragmatist. The teaching often conflicted with Leslie's Christian beliefs.

The professor's suave and gracious manner trapped many students. Leslie, however, on an examination reproduced Bode's teaching and then expressed his own position. When his examination paper was returned, Leslie found the notation, "Good—better go slow." But he got an A for the course.

During the first year out of the army he cleared up his language requirements by passing examinations in German and French. But he found no direction on his doctoral research. That would come later at the University of Iowa.

Greenville College offered Leslie the position of registrar and professor of psychology and education. The pay was $750.00 a year plus room and board. He accepted.

And there he met Lila.

She was a senior student appointed by the president as assistant to the registrar. Lila Lucile Thompson had attended Central College in McPherson, Kansas, for two years. She then had come to Greenville as a transfer student in 1919. Leslie wrote in his journal:

> Lila was attractive, and I, a bachelor of twenty-six years, was vulnerable. By the time of the Christmas vacation, I had developed a rather special interest in her—probably augmented by the attentions a young instructor was showing her which provided me the stimulus to tease her. The instructor was of Spanish blood and, although not yet a liberal arts graduate, was her Spanish instructor. "Romance language" was very properly his field! At the Christmas season he had given his students his picture, and one of them came into my possession. Miss Thompson remained in college residence during the vacation as many students did in those days before students generally commanded automobile transportation. I also stayed. Miss Thompson was seated regularly at my table in the dining room. How this all happened, I don't know. But it was acceptable to me.
>
> One day before the dining room doors had opened, I took the Spanish instructor's picture and attached it to the under-

side of Lila's water glass, picture side up. Since she was seated on the same side of the table and not immediately next to me, I missed the opportunity to witness the full impact of my joke. In lifting the glass to her lips, her full gaze met the face of the Spanish instructor. She sat the glass down and signaled a waiter, thinking that the picture was in the glass and not fastened to the bottom. And I saw the haughty indignation she exhibited. I have found by subsequent incidents also that she is often most attractive when indignant!

It was a rather uneasy afternoon for me. Although vacation, there was work she could do and normally would have done. But she did not appear. Finally, I purchased a box of candy and sent it to her with my card, inscribing thereon, "Please forgive." Well, it was not long before we were in the current and headed for the rapids. On February 16, we were engaged. Quick work!

They first planned to marry at commencement time. Leslie was under contract to teach in the department of psychology at the University of Illinois during the summer. They could go there as husband and wife. But Lila finally concluded she should go home to her mother for the eight weeks Leslie would teach. The mail between Urbana and McPherson told of their love and their plans. In a letter dated June 9, 1921, Lila discussed moving the wedding date up one day and asked when he would arrive.

She acknowledged receiving ". . . the Scripture reading" from him and gave him a list for the next week. They apparently read the same Scripture each day. Lila's letters clearly showed her love for Leslie:

July 29, 1921
My dear Leslie:
. . . I am so proud of you. You are *too* as good as I think you are. Pardon me for disputing your word, but I know you are just the best in *all* the world for *me.* . . . I love you so much and you are so good to me. You have spoiled me.

July 31, 1921
My dear Leslie:
. . . Leslie, I suppose you got my picture yesterday. Now I

suppose you will have a display of pictures on your dresser. Yes, Leslie, whenever your desires are as easily gratified as that one, they shall always be. No matter if they are harder I will try and do as you wish. It is a pleasure to do things for you. Darling, I love you so much. . . . I feel it is a great honor to be your little wife. Leslie, I am getting good and anxious.

. . . Yes, this is a wonderful, wonderful world since we have found the choice of our lives, and we are so happy in each other's love. . . .

Two weeks from now, dear, you will be with me, won't be very long—will it? I am cheered up. Don't worry about me, Sweetheart. I am happy to be your bride. Oceans of love to my Leslie.

August 3, 1921
Dearest one:

Yes, dear, I will meet you at the train. I want to. Then if you wish you can go to the YMCA. They have nice rooms there I think. I would like you to stay here, but perhaps it will look better not to, and since you prefer it, that is the way it shall be. . . .

Even in those days Leslie kept what he called, "My Line A Day." In his letters to Lila he would look back and say, "Thirty weeks ago tonight we ate dinner together as 1920 died." Or, "Seven weeks ago my first letter from Lila." Leslie's letters carried his full devotion to her:

July 29, 1921
My dearest Lila:

. . . Your picture came this morning. And thank you, oh, so much. . . . You are looking at me as I sit at my library table. . . . Two weeks from tonight—two weeks from right now, 5:07 p.m.—I shall very likely be only a few miles out of McPherson. Yes, dear, meet me at the station. You are too wonderful for me. God is good. . . .

From your letter this morning, I take it you are rather worried about many cares. Trust a bit. If we are calm and composed, everything will come out just right. Don't you believe it? . . .

August 3, 1921

. . . I love you so much and I'm so happy these days. Only ten days now. So much to do. . . . It's difficult to tell you in writing, when so soon I will be with you, that I love you. Aren't you glad our meeting next week isn't for a brief visit and then another separation? Soon the work of the summer session will be over.

For Leslie the weeks had passed slowly. At the close of the term, members of the department faculty helped him grade papers so he could get on his way to McPherson. The six hundred miles from Urbana, Illinois, to McPherson, Kansas, seemed long and slow.

He arrived two days before the wedding. With proper decorum he put up at the YMCA. The wedding took place in the new, large Thompson home on August 16, 1921. For their honeymoon they went to his parents' home in Blanchard, Michigan. Then they returned to Greenville to set up housekeeping.

They had less than $100.00 when they reached Greenville. But Leslie's situation had improved. Promoted to dean of the college, he now would receive $1200.00 for the year. They rented a furnished house, for they could not buy furniture. Another young couple, Paul and Ruth Hamilton, shared it with them. Leslie acted as head of the household the first year, Paul the second. It worked.

On their first New Year's Day together, Leslie and Lila wrote resolutions for 1922:

New Year's Resolutions
Joint Resolutions—Lila and Leslie
Resolved:
1. To strive more faithfully to attain our ideal of married life by mutual reports of the day each evening.
2. To strive to spend one hour in each other's society each day continuing our courtship.
3. To recognize God more fully in our family life.

Personal Resolutions—Leslie
Resolved:
1. To be more diligent in my secret prayer life.
2. To avoid unnecessary concerns.

   3. To be better to Lila (always to bid her "good-bye.")
   4. To bear in mind my personal relationship to those
      about me (not to become too "professionalized.")

Personal Resolutions—Lila
Resolved:
   1. To be more diligent in my secret prayer life.
   2. To use better language.
   3. To quit worrying about minor affairs.
   4. To devote one hour a day to reading of a general and
      cultural nature.
   5. To be less critical of others' failures.

The marriage of Leslie and Lila Marston worked. They brought
different attributes to the union. He soared to the heights of intellectual achievement. She was a planner and managed the home
well.

Their love bound them together and helped them weather the
differences. Leslie said it in a letter he wrote 23 years later:

November 10, 1944
Warren, Ohio
My dearest Sweetheart:
   For some time I have been feeling the urge to write a love
letter to someone—and decided on you! Not unusual, when
you so fill my mind and stir my heart. Strange at fifty I
should be sentimental? Well, nearly twenty-four years ago I
picked a flower that wouldn't droop and fade. Sometimes I
haven't watered the flower enough or given it the tender
care under which it best thrives. I am so sorry! But I am
going to give it more attention and love. I know it will respond.
   The years ahead of us can be so rich and full—if we will
have them so. We were meant for each other—down deep,
beneath all of life's tensions and surface storms—there is the
commingling current of our lives, one stream. And they will
not separate. We were kept for each other—miraculously, it
would seem. . . .
   How I marvel that I have you! And nothing but the unexpected would have jarred me out of my ivory tower—jarred

me, as did you, to the roots of my nature; jarred me to the realization of the flesh-and-blood rooting of my nature. That realization was a crisis with me—I hardly knew myself, and feared that what you stirred and wrenched loose in the depths of my being was almost wicked.

Roots in the physical, yes! And I had to learn that. But flowering in the ideal. The meaning of it all is essentially spiritual.

By the earthquake of mighty, physical love which you alone had ever wrought in me, my inhibited energies were released, extroverted. I am one of the most extreme examples of all my observation of an altered personality. I changed my direction under the impact of a woman then weighing barely a hundred pounds. . . .

Leslie showed how much he needed Lila's encouragement in another letter he wrote—which revealed that their marriage had a normal amount of rough spots. But their love prevailed and each built up the other:

My dear Lila love:

The train carrying me rapidly away from the woman I love—and for seven long weeks. Such a heavy heart I've had. Couldn't pull myself together and attack my work.

I wish we might have had a quiet hour together before I left—and I hear you say that I could have had it if I wanted it. I know you, too, are heavy-hearted, and I hope your cold and all will not get you down. My grief has been the blacker that I have hurt you so. And when I think of preaching to others that they may be "bigger than anything that can happen to them," through the power of Christ, I haven't much to say.

Since two weeks ago Monday I have been sadly "out-of-gear." For your sake, and my sake, and the work's sake, I must have assurance of your forgiveness, and God's. Can you forgive me? And then help me with myself and my work with your sweet encouragement and appreciation? For if you do not believe in me and in what I am trying to do, it's going to be pretty hard for me to repair and keep my grip. . . .

A later letter from Leslie to Lila shows their continuing love:

July 20, 1954

. . . Thirty-three years together! A third of a century! *And it lasts.* Let's make this the best of our lives—the years ahead. Financially we are as secure as the economy allows; our children are "on their own." Our health is good, in general. The Lord has been wonderful to us. And we have His work to do. The rest is up to us, isn't it? As I wrote you a few days ago, we need to relax, be easy with each other, play together, enjoy each other more. We have tended to be too tense, to "load up" with cares when we ought to trust more. I intend to try more to please you, and we'll really enjoy thinking more of each other's pleasure—even in little things. I know I can improve! I want your days to be happier and easier. . . .

Miss Lila Lucile Thompson at about the time Leslie discovered her at Greenville.

The wedding took place in the Thompson home in Mc-
Pherson, Kansas, August 16, 1921. After a Michigan
honeymoon, they set up housekeeping in Greenville, Illinois in a rented, furnished house.

The happy newlyweds. When they
began their first year together, Leslie also took up other responsibilities as dean of Greenville College.

5

Marston Makes Waves in Child Psychology

During the year following his marriage, Leslie Marston corresponded with the University of Iowa and registered for work at the Child Welfare Station at the University for the summer. He received some compensation for operating a planograph, measuring the areas of wrist bones of children's X rays taken at different ages. He said, "It was not a thrilling occupation, but it did help financially." Lila went to the University with him and took work in zoology to help her in her part-time teaching in the high school department of Greenville College.

Leslie studied at the University three summers and arranged for a one-semester leave from his position as dean at Greenville to complete his doctorate. The course he followed had its roots in his own personality, and it was influenced by his undergraduate and graduate work as well as his army experiences.

At that time, psychologists taught that personality was entirely related to intelligence, considering emotions unimportant to conduct. They believed that a child does wrong either because he knows no better or because he lacks sufficient intelligence to control his instincts and emotions.

Leslie had an internal "laboratory" that tested this theory and rejected it. While he possessed high intelligence (as his grades and other achievements demonstrated), he knew his emotions affected his actions. He was a "bashful kid from the wilds of Michigan." His learning had not released him from his shyness, though it did help him to overcome it.

He credited Lila with a major role in helping him change his personality. But the fact that he wrote so fully about it would seem to indicate that his victory was one of attitude and behavior rather than basic emotional change.

An excerpt from a letter he wrote to Lila several years later clearly showed his continuing fear of failure and need for positive reinforcement:

> . . . I've told you only a little of the terrific struggles of my earlier years against the sense of failure. I do not want those days to return at my age—it would be tragic for all of us. I need you to have confidence in me—then if I fail, I won't fail. I'm not set up like you—you seem to be bearing constant strain and tension—and are adjusted to anxiety day by day. But I can't carry it; when its gets through my defense of courage and calm, I too easily break down—or should I say "blow up"? I can sympathize with you and love you the more tenderly when you have *your* problems, but when you get worried over *my* problems—well, perhaps I haven't enough confidence in myself to carry it. . . .

Leslie Marston's recognition of his own deep needs does not take anything away from his greatness. Perhaps it adds something. His triumph over the tendency not to try made possible achievements far beyond the ordinary.

He did not stop with what he saw within himself. He set out to prove, first by reason and then by scientific research, that character and temperament must be considered along with intelligence in the evaluation of personality. That he, an intellectual, should so respond to the extreme intellectualism of his day showed both his integrity and his need for understanding of himself. He would not accept a statement of belief he considered wrong even though it would give prominence to his intelligence. He needed to prove to himself and to the world that intellect alone cannot measure the worth of a person.

His honors thesis at Greenville College had dealt with religious mysticism. Writing on "Mysticism's Message to Our Age," he endeavored to show nonintellectual dimensions of life.

For his master's thesis at the University of Illinois, Leslie had studied emotional or feeling response to literature. He used the Urbana City High School as his laboratory. His army experiences had also provided opportunities to study the relationship of emotions to personality:

> During the war, I had been engaged first with the emotionally disturbed in the psychiatric ward of Camp Custer Base Hospital, and then. . .I transferred to the camp psychologist's office where, as one of the examining and scoring staff and as chief clerk, I was directly involved with the significance of intelligence to life adjustment. . . .
>
> We were engaged, as a side interest of our primary purpose, in research on the relationship of mental level to vocation. Our charts clearly disclosed the mental superiority of the average scores of professional personnel and, descending through skilled craftsmen, to unskilled labor. Nevertheless, I reacted against the intellectualism then prevalent and was convinced that the emotional, instinctive, and generally dynamic relationships were equally if not more important. . . .
>
> At the University of Iowa, I made several ventures to locate and define an approach to the emotions, and finally decided upon a study of children's reactions to a controlled situation, the control unsuspected by the child, in terms of the direction of their energies outward upon the environment or inward upon themselves.

The results of this study became his doctoral dissertation. It was published by the University of Iowa in June 1925.* Dr. Bird T. Baldwin, Director of the Iowa Child Welfare Research Station, wrote the foreword to the book:

> In this monograph, . . . Doctor Marston has formulated an experimental approach to the study of certain nonintellectual personality traits by means of an original rating scale and five experimental test situations. In the effort to obtain a better understanding of the mechanisms conditioning children's emotional reactions, his main objective has been "to determine to what extent young children's reactions to their envi-

---

*Marston, L. R., *The Emotions of Young Children,* University of Iowa, 1925. Doctoral dissertation based on behavioral studies Marston made with children while working on his doctoral program at the University of Iowa. The book received wide acclaim for his findings. See Appendix I.

ronment, particularly social, are conditioned by constant tendencies to introversion and extroversion." . . .

The practical implication of the study is that many pronounced tendencies which may later cause maladjustment of
the child in social life are modifiable and subject to training
during the early years. . . .

Leslie Marston's published dissertation hit the academic world
like a global earthquake. He had proved by scientific methods the
error of accepted psychological suppositions. The shock waves
jarred both psychologists and sociologists. His book was quoted
and appeared in bibliographies of leading writers. And the waves
did not stop until they had changed the basic concepts of personality.

Dr. W. Richard Stephens, currently president of Greenville College and a recognized authority on the history of education, has
evaluated the work of Dr. Marston in relation to the trends of his
day:

> What was going on in American society in terms of
> thought about the nature of man during the time Marston
> was being schooled at the University of Illinois and the Uni-
> versity of Iowa was a great watershed period. John B. Wat-
> son was a great spokesman for the view that the human
> being is simply a mass of protoplasm that is shaped by cer-
> tain stimulus patterns—stimulus, response, stimulus, re-
> sponse. Thorndyke before him had even reduced it to the
> nerve endings, teaching that learning occurs where they link
> up. When that happens the human organism is shaped into
> habit patterns. So you have a very mechanistic view of the
> human being.
>
> Marston comes right out of that era, along with a few oth-
> ers. But Marston was the principal leader, saying, "Wait a
> minute. There's another dimension to man."*

A letter to his mother, written during his work on his doctorate,
reveals some details of Marston's inner self—and attributes much
of his success to his parents:

---

*Fifteen years after Dr. Marston did his work, Otto Klineberg described the first and
perhaps the most significant of the five experiments in his book, *Social Psychology,*
Henry Holt and Company, 1940, page 430. Marston's four other major experiments are also described in Appendix I.

May 10, 1923, Greenville, Illinois
Dear Mother:

The usual custom is to write to mother on Mother's Day, but I want you to have the letter to read on Mother's Day. Not simply because it is expected at this season, but because I feel it in my heart. I want to tell you that I love you, and that I attribute to you and Father my success, such as it is.

I realize my weaknesses and doubt very much if I would have "gone through" alone, as many young fellows are obliged to do who have parents far better able to assist them than mine. You have made it possible for me to employ my own powers and capabilities without being handicapped by serious financial problems.

I am glad, among other reasons, for your sakes, that I have succeeded in a measure and, I hope, have in part compensated for your sacrifice. It gives me some pleasure to enable you to think of a son who holds one of the most important positions in the church [dean of Greenville College], however small the position seems to the worldly ambitious or however little the church itself esteems it. I know it gives you some satisfaction to know that there are inviting openings in other fields if I would enter them, and I am glad that you are satisfied with my choice.

But, Mother dear, if I had not succeeded, if I were a wreck of a man—a failure—still I know where I could find sympathy and love—it's all the same to a mother.

God bless you on this day and make your heart rejoice in the love, gratitude and honor of your children. . . .I'll speak for [brother] Edd, too—he feels it but will not speak it.

The recognition that came to Dr. Marston for his innovative work brought a flood of job offers, including ones from Columbia University and the University of Chicago. The first came from the University of Iowa, as he explained in a letter to his parents not long after successfully defending his dissertation and receiving his Ph.D. in child psychology.

May 26, 1925, Greenville, Illinois
Dear folks at home:

I am sorry that I haven't written you sooner about my success at Iowa City. But no news can't be very bad news. I made it o.k. and am in great demand at Iowa City for next year. A fine job—$3,000.00 and house, heated, etc. Considering Iowa City rents, the salary would run near $3,500.00. The job would lead to something better, too.

But when I returned to Greenville, I found that the University had reported on the inspection their committee had made two weeks ago, and by that report the work of my office was praised in a very special way.

Greenville is to receive better recognition at the University. It is quite generally acknowledged that the victory is due in no small part to the dean, and the feeling that I have not labored here for nothing these five years encourages me to stay with it longer. . . .

Leslie R. Marston became Dr. Leslie R. Marston by earning a Ph.D. in child psychology at the University of Iowa.

6

Washington, D.C.—An Opportunity for Growth

$\mathbf{D}$r. Marston continued to ignore offers of prestigious jobs as he continued his work as dean at Greenville College. For a while Dr. Baldwin* contacted him frequently about other possibilities. Leslie made it clear he intended to stay with Christian education. He heard no more until January 5, 1926.

Dr. Baldwin had also become chairman of the Child Welfare Committee of the National Research Council (NRC) in Washington, D.C. Founded in 1920, the committee functioned under the Division of Anthropology and Psychology of the NRC. It participated in several activities but struggled to find both purpose and function.

Chairman Baldwin recommended several programs that were turned down. Then in November 1924, he made a proposal that got action. He suggested extensive study to determine ". . . how far the traits and abilities of the child are determined by heredity and how far they are determined by very early environment."

The first project under the program was ". . . to assemble, classify, and make available all scientific research on children from birth to six years of age." This included the publication of 5,000 copies of the results. The Laura Spellman Rockefeller Memorial made a grant of $3,500 for the project. The committee made a start at research by circulating a questionnaire to 1,600 scholars in

---

*Dr. Baldwin was Director of the Iowa Child Welfare Research Station at the University of Iowa, and had written the foreword to Marston's doctoral dissertation, *The Emotions of Young Children.*

fields related to child welfare. The replies showed disagreement on the value of the proposed project.

Out of this floundering came the decision in December 1925 to seek the support of the Laura Spellman Rockefeller Memorial to employ an executive secretary. Eight days later Leslie received a letter from Dr. Baldwin inviting him to apply for the position.

Leslie still wasn't interested in leaving Greenville College, but he shared the letter with Dr. Burritt, president of the college. Then a regular campus event changed the direction of Dr. Marston's life. He noted in his journal:

> At about that time, following the Christmas holiday, I was assigned to lead the midweek campus prayer meeting. I did not know that the floor of the chapel had been treated with oil during the vacation. Kneeling-in-prayer devotions could not prevail, as was the custom. In its place, I called for testimonies from faculty and students concerning experiences in prayer. The results were beyond the usual and deeply affected me.
>
> Two days later it struck me with force that I had not prayed about Dr. Baldwin's request that I submit my name as a candidate for the National Research Council position in Washington. I simply took it for granted that I should remain in Christian service.
>
> As I prayed and considered the invitation, I became more and more convinced that perhaps I should submit my name.

Leslie wrote Dr. Baldwin expressing interest in the position. They arranged a meeting in St. Louis. Leslie made it clear he did not want his interest in the job to indicate a desire to leave Christian education on a permanent basis. And he could not commit himself to the four-year term the committee suggested. With Baldwin's agreement to these conditions, he submitted his application. With it he sent an excerpt from a letter that told of his success at Greenville:

> I went over in detail the scholastic records of the school with Dean Marston. I have not found better records in any of the colleges I have visited nor more conclusive evidence of a painstaking adherence to published standards. All advice to students on educational matters is handled by the dean.

Rules for probation, dropping for poor scholarship, withdrawals from courses and the like have been adopted and are made effective by him. They are not mere *paper* rules. The records show that they have been put into operation.

G. F. Tuttle, for the Committee on Admissions
from Higher Institutions of the University
of Illinois, May 19, 1925

Leslie mailed his application January 22. Then he waited. Since he had no response by March, he concluded someone else had been appointed. He wrote Dr. Baldwin and Baldwin's answer stated that no decision had been made. On Sunday, March 21, Dr. Baldwin called Leslie from Chicago. The committee was meeting. Could he come? He declined to leave on Sunday but took a train at 2:00 a.m. Monday, arriving in Chicago at 10:00 a.m. The committee voted to hire him at $4,250 per year with an annual increase of $250. He would work one-fourth time from April 1 to June 30, so he could carry on his duties at the college to the end of the school year.

This was good news to Leslie, but not to Lila. Though at first reluctant to consider the position, he was now convinced that God opened up the opportunity and directed him to take it. Lila saw it as a compromise of his commitment to Christian service. She feared he would drift away from the church and perhaps from the Lord.

His journal entry for June 16, 1926, while in Washington near the end of his part-time service, shows the breadth of their disagreement:

Received a letter from Lila in which she expresses her fear that we are making a serious mistake in leaving Greenville. My conviction is growing stronger continually that we are doing the right thing. She is so afraid of endorsing the move that she will not commend accomplishment or rejoice at recognition that is accorded me. Quite consistently she depreciates every apparent desirable feature of the project.

And yet from the first day I arrived on my first trip here to this moment, there has not been a single disappointing feature. On the contrary, many happy surprises. . . .

What has the next few months in store for us? I would have full confidence, if I had Lila's support. Our hope is in subordinating all to the great end, better qualifications for service in the Kingdom. But she can't see how that is possible, and her lack of faith threatens our grip on such a goal.

But I wonder if after all I am not becoming stronger by very reason of the load she throws on me because of her doubt? Truly I must "go it alone," or fail.

I must remember that her burden is greater than mine—although needlessly so.

Dr. Marston became well established in his work during this three-month's part-time service, spending one week each month in Washington during April, May, and June. Even on his first visit he had been surprised at the attention shown him in spite of his ". . . lack of standing in the profession." He learned that many had read his book, *The Emotions of Young Children,* and considered him an authority on child development.

When he returned to Greenville in June, he went by way of New York to visit the Laura Spellman Rockefeller Memorial. On the train from New York to his home in Greenville, he wrote the letter* to his parents that outlined his life and expressed his hopes for the Kingdom.

Before moving to Washington, Leslie and Lila bought their first car, an Essex. It proved to be a mixed blessing. Leslie had not driven more than 300 miles in all of his life. But he became an enthusiastic driver, typical of all his activities. On the way to Washington he drove 900 miles without car trouble after he thought he had the car cured of "jerks" caused by two fouled spark plugs. The "jerks" became a chronic ailment, but Leslie never lost his enthusiasm for driving.

Following their move to Washington in July, Lila's reluctant attitude began to change. They fellowshiped with Greenville graduates and former professors working in Washington. They worshiped at the new B. T. Roberts Memorial Church—a Free Methodist church. Lila developed a circle of friends and became involved in her own activities. This was good, for Leslie's responsibilities often took him away from home.

Once settled in Washington, he helped the committee on Child Development formulate a four-fold purpose:

1. To stimulate research in child development.
2. To correlate and integrate research activities.

---

*Chapter 1, page 13.

3. To disseminate research information.

4. To facilitate contacts between research personnel.

A paper Leslie presented to the committee in October 1926 showed the activities carried on in line with the purposes:

> To these ends, the Executive Secretary is now preparing a research directory on child development covering all phases of child research, physical and mental. The directory will be issued in November or December. . . .
>
> A list of unpublished bibliographies on child development is also in preparation, and will be issued in a few months. . . .
>
> The committee also summons conferences on child research from time to time as appropriations therefore can be secured. . . .
>
> The committee also advertises the National Research Fellowships in Child Development, which are supported by the Laura Spellman Rockefeller Memorial, receives applications for same, and recommends appointments to the Memorial. . . .

Dr. Marston's journal, reports to the committee, and minutes of meetings show a heavy work load as well as ". . . association with world-known scientists." The preparation of the research directory was hard work, but rewarding. It gave him an understanding of the field that made him an authority on the subject. The conferences which he directed gave him personal contact with leaders in child development.

Administration of the fellowships in child development probably most enhanced his standing with educators. When he visited the campuses of Columbia, Yale, Harvard, Cornell, the University of Iowa, and other leading educational institutions, he found a warm welcome. His recommendation would largely determine how many fellowships the school would receive. His book and his ability commended him to all he met. The committee gave him high praise.

All of this made him sought after as a speaker and a leader. He spoke to such diverse groups as the government Bureau of Home Economics, the National Conference on Nursery Schools, the Conference on Research in Child Development, the Midwestern Conference of the School of Education of the University of Kansas, the Rural Club of Columbia University, and various church services. On April 16, 1927, he wrote in his journal, ". . . . I am busy for a few days with my speech making. . . . All good training, but hard work for one not a natural born orator."

Another part of the same entry shows his growing stature:

> When I arrived at the dinner of the Nursery School Con-
> ference two weeks ago, I learned that the other speaker was
> John B. Watson, the leader of behaviorism. I was over-
> whelmed at the contrast and distressed that I was quoting
> him in my paper, opposing a research plan he had pro-
> posed. Reverberations of criticism of his speech that evening
> continue to the present, but the next day I was elected a
> member of the committee of the nursery school leaders. The
> crowd was enthusiastic.

Others sought Leslie's leadership. When three government agencies, two universities, and three independent organizations formed the Washington Child Development Center, they elected him chairman of the executive committee. He was made an advisory editor of a new magazine, *Children*.

Dr. Baldwin asked him to teach one hour a day for six weeks at the University of Iowa. Leslie refused but finally agreed to five lectures in one week. While there they treated him as a VIP. Lunches, dinners, outings, and a tea in his honor filled his free time. There was no doubt about it. Dr. Leslie R. Marston had gained national renown.

The Marstons ready to embark on their move to Washington, D.C. The car was a 1926 Essex, the first he had ever owned.

Since the last writing we have moved to historic George-town, Apartment 232, New Gardens. We are directly off the Garden in the quad-rangle, which has been most beautiful this fall. I am much nearer my work now, and come home for lunch, relieving somewhat Lila's lonesomeness.

A section from Leslie Marston's journal describes their move to historic Georgetown in Washington, D.C.

The photo shows Lila in the garden area of their new residence.

The Greenville College board elected
Leslie Marston president in September, 1927, so their residence in
Washington, D.C., lasted only a little
more than one year.

7

The New President
of Greenville College

On August 26, 1927, Dr. E. G. Burritt, President of Greenville College, died. Dr. Marston attended the funeral. While there Mrs. Burritt confided in him that her husband had wanted Leslie to succeed him. This, of course, could not determine the matter, but it did represent a concensus shared by many that Marston was the man.

When Leslie had left Greenville College in 1926, he saw his new work with the National Research Council as serving "... a big purpose in the Kingdom." He had longed for Lila to see the experience as providing "... better qualifications for the Kingdom." And that attitude stayed with him as shown by his journal entry the following January. "I find my position [here at NRC] everything I had hoped, excepting the opportunity for library research and writing. However, the pull to Christian work is strong, and one more year will satisfy me."

The board of Greenville College elected Dr. Marston president on the first ballot on September 6, 1927. He responded with a telegram withholding his decision and asking for a meeting with the executive committee of the board on Friday, September 9. Thursday morning he and Lila left for Greenville by car. They arrived in time for the meeting where he accepted the position. Now President Marston, he stayed in Greenville two weeks to get the school year started.

During this time they moved into the president's home and wired Lila's sister, Sylvia, to come to stay with Lila who had not been well for several months. Their longing for a family had promise of gratification, but the prospects were not so bright for Lila at that date.

For the next five months Dr. Marston shuttled between Greenville and Washington while his successor at the National Research Council was chosen and trained. His first return to Greenville following the election had been especially eventful:

> I drove to Greenville on the return trip, moving such of our possessions as the car could carry. I left Washington at 9:00 a.m. Tuesday, October 18. A rainy, miserable day. In the Cumberland Mountains I struck a heavy snow—probably twelve inches, which packed against the windshield. The windshield wipers could clear but a small spot, so thick, heavy and wet was the snow. I drove much of the way through the mountains in second gear. Descending the last mountain into Uniontown, my gears slid into neutral as I was about to pass a truck. The car shot ahead, but I swung toward the wall side of the mountain and applied the emergency brake, stopping safely. I admit that I prayed.
>
> That night I put up in Washington, Pennsylvania. The next day I suffered the first flat tire of my driving experience. A few minutes after repairs, I burned out a bearing, probably through oil-line defect. From 1:30 p.m. to 7:00 p.m. the car was in a garage for repairs. I pushed on until nearly midnight when I stopped at a tourist camp between Springfield, Ohio, and Dayton. The next day I lost several hours from oil-line trouble, generator trouble, and distributor trouble. However, I reached home about 10:00 p.m. Thursday.

Another time President Marston returned home because of a happy emergency. It didn't appear happy at first. In the early morning of February 6, the telephone in his room at the Powhaton Hotel awakened him. The caller related the message of a telegram. Lila was ill. He should come at once. The news gave him concern. The baby should not arrive for another month. The terseness of the telegram made it easy for him to think the worst. He rushed by taxi through the darkness to his office to put a few things in order. Another taxi took him across the city to the railway station. After buying a ticket and before the train departed, he decided to call home.

Lila's sister answered the telephone with the news that he was the father of a baby girl. She and her mother were doing well. Would he approve Evelyn Lucile for the baby's name? He did. Then he did something typically Marston:

> Since all was going so well we agreed that I spend the day in Washington and set my office in shape to leave on the "America" the following afternoon to arrive in Greenville ten hours later than the train I had planned to take. . . .
>
> I arrived home Thursday, February 8, at 4:00 p.m. Lila and baby were doing well indeed. The baby was small but perfect—brown hair and blue eyes. The students reported that the first hour she said, "mama," the second, "papa," the third, "psychology."

*   *   *

Family tradition relates another event connected with Marston's return to Greenville. In 1925, he had written an article for *Psychological Clinic* based on his study of the causes of Mongolism (now called Down's Syndrome). His research had revealed two widely accepted causes that gave him concern now. This severe mental deficiency occurred in babies born to women who suffered illness during pregnancy. It also afflicted first babies of women older than average. Lila fit both descriptions. She had been ill and she was thirty-two years old, somewhat above the average age for a first pregnancy.

According to the legend, when Dr. Marston returned home he went up the back stairs and into the nursery. He carefully examined Evelyn, both for facial characteristics of Mongoloids and for bone structure considered indicative of the disorder. She passed the inspection. Satisfied, he went to see Lila.

*   *   *

By the end of February, the shift to the presidency was complete. Dr. Marston plunged into the work of the college with the same vigor that had characterized his previous activities. But he had a new advantage. When dean of the college, he had had a favorable reputation based on the publication of his dissertation. Now he had the additional prestige gained by his effective work at the National Research Council and his "... association with world-known scientists ..." and leaders in education. If he had stayed at Greenville instead of taking the Washington job, he undoubtedly would have been elected president. But now he brought more experience and broader knowledge to the position.

Dr. Marston wrote in his journal on January 2, 1928:

> I have wondered at times if I have done the best thing in returning to Greenville. I am staking my all on Greenville and have faith in success, but heavy loads are to be borne. I know by experience already. Providence has pointed clearly this direction, and I shall do my best. Greenville is poor in material resources but rich in "personability"—faculty and students. My ambition is to make the college genuinely liberal arts.

Dr. Marston kept his commitment to make Greenville College a strong influence. He began by giving the college excellent leadership. Everyone knew who was in charge and they liked it. Then he led in the formation of a philosophy of education for the college.

The Inaugural Challenge

At Dr. Marston's inauguration on April 26, 1928, he spoke on "The Christian Ideal in Education."*

He climaxed his address by setting forth eight guiding principles that flow out of the Christian ideal in education. This summary gives the essence of them:

1. Since all experience educates, education is never completed.
2. The Christian college recognizes the central place of education in the religious life of the individual and in the Kingdom of God.
3. The Christian college follows the principle that true education is essentially a change of heart that brings the individual into adjustment with God.
4. The product of the Christian college should be Christian character.
5. The Christian college regards all worthy objectives of educa-

---

*The major concepts of Dr. Marston's address are presented in Appendix II.

tion as means to this end of adjustment to God.

6. The purpose of the Christian college is not to train persons how to make a living, but how to live.

7. The task of Christian teachers, whatever their specialties, is to train their students how to live.

8. Since all experience educates, extra-curricular activities, when kept in proper relationships, are part of the educational process.

The new president's final words gave the reason for the existence of Greenville College and pointed the direction it should go:

> Therefore, in view of the considerations of the hour and this concluding summary of guiding principles, the Christian college is not a cloistered retreat from the problems of a changing world to the seclusion of which a few monkish professors withdraw to create, unchecked by the restrictions of reality, an ideal world of fixed forms and values to which they fit the minds of students likewise seeking release from the demands of a changing order. Neither is the Christian college the last feeble stand of a dying orthodoxy, the expiring protest of a lost cause. Rather it is at the axle of the world's thought; it seeks the fullest expression of truth; it is a foremost experiment on the frontier of educational advance.

*   *   *

Dr. W. Richard Stephens, Greenville's current president, indicates that this final statement from Dr. Marston's inaugural address, though made half a century ago, ". . . is yet today the freshest, most cogent and challenging statement regarding the purpose and mission of the Christian liberal arts college."

*   *   *

Dr. Marston's inaugural address was the Magna Carta for the rebirth of Greenville College. He did not depreciate what previous presidents had done. As a graduate he demonstrated the adequacy of their leadership. But he gave the college new dimensions for growth and service.

He expanded its horizon to include the whole spectrum of educational endeavor. He gave it depth with the challenge to train persons how to live. He gave it height by defining and implementing the Christian ideal in education. And he gave the college a yardstick to measure its success: the building of Christian character.

Leslie Marston brought recognition to Greenville College because of his wide acceptance in educational circles. When Marston talked, educators listened. In a rural county seat of less than 5,000 people in southern Illinois, fifty miles east of St. Louis, now lived and worked one of the leading educational experts of America. His greatness enhanced everything he touched.

An original pen-and-ink drawing of Hogue Hall, Greenville College. It is unsigned, but is thought to have been done by Leslie Marston.

8

The Great Depression vs. Survival of Greenville

During the 1920s, American religious, business, and political leaders talked about the "New Era." They proclaimed continuing economic growth, full employment, freedom from war, and the elimination of poverty.

They received good response from their optimistic message. Many followed the rainbow that promised riches for all. The get-rich-quick psychology led them into high risk investments. The buying of stocks became brisk, then speculative, often done with borrowed money.

The rainbow faded on "Black Thursday," October 24, 1929. As stock prices plummeted, a group of bankers managed to halt the drop with expressions of confidence and the infusion of money. But on "Tragic Tuesday," October 29, the market collapsed. Crumbling prices swept away billions of dollars. The wealth of millionaires and the savings of working men disappeared together.

Politicians and businessmen tried to play down the effects of the crash. News stories and editorials spoke of the temporary nature of the problem. Manufacturers kept wages up in the hope that spending by workers would bring recovery. But the market collapse had destroyed much of the capital of the nation. This left businesses, large and small, without resources for operation and expansion. The economy was on a downhill slide, but it took about three years to hit bottom.

The *New York Times* covered the crash of the market without a hint of the impending Depression. Not until 1932 did the depths of the calamity appear on its pages. By then it wasn't news. With unemployment on the rise, businesses failing, and banks closing, millions of Americans were caught in the downward spiral. By 1933, unemployment rose to 25 percent of the work force. Those who had jobs took cuts in wages and hours. Jury duty at $4.00 a day was sought after. And so was jail, with a place to sleep and something to eat.

The "New Era" of the 1920s had not meant much to farmers and coal miners. They had not shared in the prosperity and optimism of the day. Depressed before the Depression, the financial collapse had pushed them down all the more.

Since Greenville College was surrounded by farms and local coal mines, it felt the impact of a double depression. But as with the nation, the financial decline was gradual rather than sudden.

During the closing hours of 1928, Dr. Marston did some catch-up work on his journal. He wrote of new laboratories, drawing boards for pre-engineering students, and improvements to the library. Obviously, Greenville College was moving ahead. But one sentence speaks of the depression before the Depression: "Registration is a little lower this year—due to financial depression very likely."

He did not mention the Depression again until January 14, 1932, when he wrote: "The severe financial depression creates an emergency, but we are not facing a crisis as are so many schools."

Some of those other schools appear in his journal later. He wrote of one college with wonderful campus and buildings, but with a debt of a half-million dollars. Later he reported that the president of that college was in the hospital with a heart attack due to the financial load. Another college faced the question of whether it could open. It did by raising $5,000 to meet obligations. Yet another went into bankruptcy, paying only three cents on the dollar to creditors.

Dr. Marston explained Greenville's situation in his journal on August 26, 1933: "For several weeks I have been busy on the campus. One of my first tasks was raising money to meet most pressing obligations."

*   *   *

Greenville College did better than many other institutions during the Depression, due largely to two special programs inaugurated by President Marston. The fact that these were not academic endeavors shows he could apply his creativity to needs of most any nature.

First, the college needed students. A college faces a double problem here. Without students there can be no school, so the college cannot fulfill its purpose. And students bring money. Average charges of only $230 per semester for tuition, books, fees, room, board, and miscellaneous costs in 1932 provided income essential for the operation of the school. With the economy down, fewer young people could afford college. The Depression threatened both the purpose and the funding of Greenville.

President Marston began working from within toward a solution to the economic problems of the college. At a meeting of the college board on June 3, 1932, a committee of the faculty presented a statement expressing the faculty's willingness to share in the risk of reduced enrollment. This included getting new students and voluntary gifts to help balance the budget. "We assume obligation," the statement said, ". . . for the amount by which the financial campaign fails to realize the $3,800 now needed to balance the budget."

But his major thrust was outward. He offered his services to high schools for a "School and Community Day" and sent along a biographical sketch. That, with his broad recognition in educational circles, brought enthusiastic response. He gave his own appraisal of the project in his journal:

> I am developing an extensive promotional campaign to put Greenville "on the map" in central and southern Illinois. Our students come largely from outside the state, but beginning at its doors there is an area covering 12,000 square miles in Illinois with no liberal arts college. With Miss Olive Van Valin, a marvelous soprano on our music staff, I am putting on a "School and Community Day" in many of the surrounding leading communities.
>
> The plan is winning excellent cooperation from high school principals, and I am getting a hearing before Rotary Clubs, high schools, brotherhoods, and other groups. We began our program last week at West Frankfort, a community of 15,000 with a high school of over 1,000. Our schedule included:
> Rotary luncheon: "This Business of Education"
> High school assembly: "Managing Our Emotions"

Women's club: "Managing Our Emotions"
Parents' meeting: "How Queer Folk Get That Way"
[*Queer* had no sexual connotations then.]
Later in the week we put on programs before the high schools of Bridgeport and Lawrenceville and the Lawrenceville Rotary Club. . . . In these three days in the field, we had a hearing of over 2,000 people. And we are now scheduled for Pana, Flora, Fairfield, Leansboro, Mt. Carmel, Pickneyville, and Centralia. Other communities are to be scheduled. Hard work! But important.

Putting the college on the map helped, but it did not solve all the problems of getting students. It developed more prospects, but it did not provide the money to pay their expenses.

This led to President Marston's second project—student employment.

First came Tower Products, named for the tower on the main campus building. Tower Press was launched at the meeting of the college Board of Trustees on June 3, 1932. For $3,500, the Press bought sufficient equipment to set up an adequate print shop. Friends of the college interested in the Press loaned the money. The finances were kept separate from the regular college funds. The Press operated successfully into the 1960s, doing college printing at reduced cost, taking in outside work, and making it possible for the students who worked there to pay their college expenses.

The same June 1932 meeting of the Board of Trustees received a recommendation from President Marston that the college ". . . operate industry to supply employment to aid students in financing their education in this institution, such industries to consist of steam laundry, printing shop, farm, store, manufacturing and sale of chemicals, toilet articles, and general merchandise. . . ."

Not all these programs developed, but Tower Products became a major student employment industry. Dr. H. J. Long, whom President Marston recruited to teach chemistry, developed a line of flavorings, household cleansers, and cosmetics. Students manufactured and sold the products. Under the name, "Collegiate Products," other colleges sold them in their bookstores.

Pre-college young people sold Tower Products to build up personal scholarship funds on which the college paid five percent interest. The success of the venture led to the appointment of Dr.

Long to the position of executive assistant to the president, with specific tasks of directing student finances, including student employment.

Professor Harriet Whiteman, for years a member of the college faculty, remembers Tower Products from the inside:

> When I was a student, my title was Publicity Secretary. I used to work at a little table in the room called the faculty lounge, but actually an annex to Dr. Marston's office. I have vivid memories of Dr. Marston and Dr. Long sitting near Dr. Marston's desk, both with their feet up on the desk as they were deep in plans about various kinds of promotional schemes. One of the liveliest was Tower Products. Several prominent business people got their start selling Tower Products door to door. In the depths of the Depression, Tower Products was parallel to "Avon Calling." Confidentially, the face powder always turned orange. I never had any trouble with the toothpaste.
>
> A number of young fellows of my student generation earned their way through school selling Tower Products. They sold during the summer as well as the school year. It was also good public relations for the college.

Greenville College did more than just survive the Depression. Strong but wholesome promotion and the student employment program aided both the college and the students. These special efforts helped Greenville College avoid calamities faced by many colleges. While most college enrollments were declining, Greenville College registration went from 232 in 1931-32 to 252 in 1933-34. It dropped to 235 by the 1935-36 academic year, still above 1931-32.

During this time the academic ratings of the college continued to rise. In 1930, the University of Illinois, the accrediting institution for colleges in Illinois at that time, raised Greenville from a basic C to a basic B with a qualified A. Students especially recommended to the University could enter on an A rating. President Marston wrote in his journal: "This is a great step forward, justifying our policy of improving faculty certification, equipment—especially in laboratories and library—and increasing our income by systematic field work."

Four years later, Dr. Marston attended a meeting of a new accrediting association, about which he noted: "April 19-20 to the North Central meeting Chicago, to learn more about the new movement toward qualitative standards. Enthused! Have since organized a committee of the faculty on Institutional Survey with Mrs. Woods a paid part-time secretary!"

The resulting actions—together with the program of overall improvement—led to accredited membership in the new association. The college has continued to pass reexamination without question to the present day.

President Marston and Dr. H. J. Long were partners in Greenville's plan for survival. Together they were responsible for the development of "Tower Products" — a number of saleable items that were sold by students to help earn their own way, and also to help provide a modest flow of cash into the college coffers.

9

Sorrow and Joys During Greenville Presidency

Sorrow came to the Marston family during their years at Greenville College. In September 1929, Dr. Marston's mother died following a stroke and a lingering illness. When he learned of her stroke in July, Leslie and his family made a hurried trip to his parents' home in Blanchard, Michigan. They found his mother with a clear mind and good speech, and after several days he and his family returned to Greenville. His journal records developments:

> The last week in August, I was lecturing at the Lafayette County Teachers Institute when word came that Mother was worse. I secured a substitute for my last day and went home by train, arriving Thursday morning, August 29. Mother was much worse than when I had left her in July. . . . The next day her condition was less favorable, and she knew callers less clearly. . . . She passed into a coma from which she never rallied. The stupor continued for four anxious days and ended with death at about 7:00 p.m. Tuesday, September 3.
>
> A peaceful passing. The sun near its setting, throwing its bright beams into the chamber. Evening quiet prevailing. Father, Edd, Bertha, and I at the bedside. Mother left us.

(Dr. Marston's father died April 5, 1941, but no journal has been found covering that period.)

Even though income was limited and the work load at Greenville was demanding, the Marston family weathered the Depression years. President Marston carried a heavy travel schedule, leaving his wife, Lila, to care for major home responsibilities.

For Dr. Marston these were years of recognition, honor, and hard work. For instance, in one year he spoke eighty-eight times to a wide variety of audiences. This load of preparation, travel, and speaking, with the responsibilities of the college during the Depression could have crushed an ordinary man. But he carried it well. And it all enhanced his standing in educational, community, and religious circles.

Early in his service as president, Dr. Marston frequently participated in child welfare and educational organizations. Often he was the principal speaker. He attended the Conference of the National Council of Parental Education. He addressed the Indiana Home Economics Association, the Farm and Home Week Conference of the University of Illinois, and the American Association of University Women. He taught summer school at the University of Michigan and the University of Iowa. And he turned down offers of lucrative positions from such institutions.

Dr. Marston's distinctions included membership in the National Scientific Honor Society of Sigma Xi, Fellow of the American Association for the Advancement of Science, and charter member of the Society for Research in Child Development.

In November 1930, he attended the White House Conference on Child Health and Protection at the invitation of President Hoover. As a member of the committee that dealt with the child in relation to institutions and the home, he had significant influence in planning the White House Conference. He served on the subcommittee of four persons that rewrote recommendations for presentation to the Conference.

*   *   *

Family events rated strongly in his journal:

AN IMPORTANT DAY
FRIDAY, JANUARY 13, 1933

Robert Vincent Marston was born—a little fellow, but perfectly formed and a handsome baby. Lila a brave little heroine. Evelyn [five years of age] received the news with great joy. Insisted that he be named Leslie Ray Marston. Finally told me, "Daddy, I'll call him Leslie Ray Marston, and you call him what you want to."

Dr. Marston's journal gleams with comments on Evelyn's development. On January 1, 1934, he wrote about her joining the church at almost six years of age at the close of an evangelistic series:

> Several joined the church at the conclusion, Evelyn among them. Our house-maid, a college student who had never been a Christian, was converted and consented to join the church. Evelyn decided she wished to join with her. Her mother and I were not fully convinced. Finally, on Sunday morning the pastor talked to her and me also. I finally told her that she was pretty young, that she had joined the Junior Missionary Society, and later she could join the church. She said in a resigned tone, "All right, but I do think that this is the time."
> Her mother and I decided to leave the matter with her. I was in the pulpit that morning, and when the pastor gave the call for those who would join the church, the student came forward and with her Evelyn Lucile. . . .

Dr. Marston liked to relate another incident involving his young daughter which occurred during his time as Greenville president:

> Evelyn, listening to a conversation in the college dining hall, had difficulty understanding how a local wedding ceremony could have been performed by a man who was not only the Marston's mail-carrier, but unknown to Evelyn, a preacher as well. A college professor, endeavoring to enlighten her said, "Don't you understand, Evelyn? Your Daddy is a college president and a preacher, too."
> Evelyn's response was, "Oh, but Daddy isn't much of a preacher!"

*   *   *

By 1934, Dr. Marston's involvement in child welfare activities had diminished. His emphasis shifted to the "School and Community" programs and the promotional work of the college. He continued his involvement with educational organizations but was less often a speaker. He more often preached at local and general meetings of his church.

In addition to all of his other activities as college president, Dr. Marston wrote a book out of the chaos of the Great Depression.* The title, *From Chaos to Character,* gave hope to the hopeless. But it carried a message deeper than economic salvation. The volume spoke of man created in the image of God but degraded by sin. Drawing on his background in psychology, Dr. Marston defined personality as a combination of intellect, temperament, and conduct. He wrote of the bankruptcy of intellectualism as the supposed answer to all of our problems. He dealt with the folly of living for thrills alone. He discussed the relationship of emotions and life. He closed a chapter on "Man, A Moral Creator," with:

> We have asserted man's freedom in this chapter, a freedom to choose and strive toward his own destiny, utilizing to that end the powers of nature working upon him through environment and in him through heredity. Thus the doctrine of freedom recognizes the claim of the law, through which alone man can achieve freedom in his own spirit, in the universe of nature, and in society. The doctrine of freedom or self-determination, we have observed, has been strengthened by new concepts in science and by the family of the old determinism in the realm of personality. But notwithstanding man's moral freedom, he is incapable of saving himself by his good works or character.

In his final chapter, "The Stature of Christ," Dr. Marston wrote:

> Man is called, not merely to save his soul and insure an eternal destiny in Heaven, but to devote his energies, his talents, all his resources in laying the foundations of his eternity. If the reader could have the guarantee of God Himself that regardless of his life and conduct for the next twenty years he would finally inherit eternal life, those twenty years would nevertheless in a vital way condition his eternal career.

---

*Marston, L. R., *From Chaos to Character,* Tower Press, 1935. Written primarily for use as a study guide for the national youth organization of the Free Methodist Church. But the book was widely acclaimed and cordially received in broad circles because of its message of hope in a hopeless world. Three editions have been printed, the last in 1948 by Light and Life Press.

We acquire here spiritual wrinkles that eternity itself can never iron out.

And thus the Christian's philosophy gives significance to this life, for the work we begin here will be consummated there. This life then becomes important! More than a dressing room for eternity, it is a laboratory of the Eternal.

With recognition in education, psychology, and child welfare, Dr. Marston enjoyed the high regard of many scholars. With his leadership in curriculum, administration, promotion, and student employment, he set a high standard for the college presidency. With his interest in the total person and his spiritual understanding, he led many to Christian commitment and a life of integrity. He surely would continue to lead Greenville College for many years.

But on August 29, 1933, he had been ordained an elder for the ministry in the Free Methodist Church, preparing the way for another change in the course of his life.

Left: Mutual joy enlivened the relationship between Evelyn and her little brother, Bobby. *Right:* President Marston with his children at the Bok Singing Tower in Florida. Travel began for the Marston family while the children were young. Evidently Lila took the photo.

The President of the United States

invites

Dr. Marston

to be a delegate to the White House

Conference on Child Health and Protection

which is called in the City of Washington

November nineteenth to twenty-second

Nineteen hundred and thirty

President Herbert Hoover sent this engraved invitation from the White House to Dr. Marston in 1930. During his year in Washington, Marston had established himself as an authority on child care and development.

10

Election "So Unusual" Surprises the Marstons

The church's clarion call to an expanded ministry is described in Dr. Marston's journal:

> My life is rushing faster than this record. Without filling in the gap following the last entry, I write the event of this day, Thursday, October 24, 1935.
>
> I am at Winona Lake, Indiana. I arrived here Monday for the annual church boards and the Association of Free Methodist Colleges. School interests and a special project on Cooperative Service Training have held me here until this time. This afternoon the Board of Administration held its election of the bishop to take the place vacated by the death last August of Bishop A. D. Zahniser. . . .
>
> At General Conference here at Winona Lake last summer, I received six complimentary votes. Several have been talking to me about the matter, usually indulging in pleasantry, and many quite seriously giving the opinion that within a few years at most I would be elected.
>
> I entered the meeting of the board, held in the publishing house chapel . . . as the first ballot was being called. Shortly after I was seated, my name was called. A little later, three or four in a row. When the results were announced, there were about twelve candidates, the highest having received six, and I followed with five. The second ballot carried me to ten; the third, to fifteen out of twenty-seven: the election—with one

to spare. . . . My head whirled as each succeeding ballot jumped my total.

So unusual!—an ordained elder only two years, a school man never pastor of a church, naturally reserved and considered "cold" by many.

The contributing factors probably include at least these three:

1. Bishop Griffith's full backing, although he is not the promoter type and certainly had not solicited votes;
2. Two members of my Greenville board who evidently gave me complimentary votes on the first ballot and stayed with me when they saw others were interested;
3. I was supply president of a Conference last August for Bishop Griffith and impressed very favorably the senior elder who is a member of the Board of Administration. When the elder had received Bishop Griffith's letter appointing me, he had been disappointed. He had the reputation for being against education. . . . I found the senior elder a splendid man to work with, one of the kindest-hearted of men on the stationing committee, but loyal to what he understood as duty. I won him! He reported to one of my friends here this week that I was one of the best "supply" presiding officers they had ever had in handling the Conference, serving on the stationing committee, addressing the Conference, and preaching. (Perhaps my friend has exaggerated the report a little.) Well, no doubt the elder had talked to enough people who voted their favorite son on the first ballot but, reassured by this man's approval of an educator, swung to me to save their vote on the later ballots.

I am now down on the edge of Warsaw [an adjacent town] eating alone, too self-conscious to go to the Westminster Hotel dining room with the crowd tonight.

I suppose Lila knows because one of the Greenville men wired his wife who would call Lila. I plan to call Lila this evening. She will be all "cut up" over the affair. She is pretty fond of Greenville. But perhaps we will move to our own home and continue to live there. At this moment, that appeals to me as the best thing to do. Perhaps the family could summer here while I make the conference rounds.

The new bishop's journal entry several days later continues the story of the events following the election:

> The Board of Administration adjourned at about midnight. I went to bed about 1:30 but did not sleep well for some time.
>
> The next morning, Friday, I left by car with Brother Lees of Cowden and J. M. Daniels for Tuscola, Illinois, where Brother Daniels and I caught a train for Hillsboro where our wives and Bobby met us.
>
> The night before I had called Lila and found her as I had expected, pretty much upset. She wanted me to resign, but I hadn't been able to get the consent of my conscience. A compelling conviction, it seemed to me, would alone justify my ignoring the call of the church.
>
> We drove to Greenville, arriving at about 5:15 p.m., to find the school gathered in a mass meeting on the athletic field. Speeches by Professor Holtwick representing the faculty, J. M. Daniels, representing the Board of Trustees, and the president of the Student Association, Ralph Miller. A speech by me, of course.

Marston's "so unusual" election to the bishopric was not as cataclysmic as it appeared. From boyhood he had had some inclination to the ministry. As a high school student he had used his father's church ". . . for my early sermonic attempts." In an old Bible he wrote alongside Jeremiah 8:22: "Text of my first sermon—1913 or 1914, 'Is there no balm in Gilead: is there no physician there? Why then is not the health of the daughter of my people recovered?' "

But the events that qualified him for election as bishop took place without his initiation and with his often reluctant consent.

The Free Methodist Church has four levels of certification and ordination for the ministry. It begins with local preacher, or lay minister. This does not always result in full-time pastoral ministry. Many continue to serve in the lay capacity as John Wesley encouraged in the early days of Methodism. But the local certification is the beginning for those who later go into full-time ministry.

The second step is admission to the annual conference "on trial" or in "preparatory membership."

After two years in this relationship comes full membership in the conference and ordination as a "traveling deacon." This entails the willingness to accept appointments to conference churches.

Two years later comes ordination as a "traveling elder," all of this with stipulated educational and practical requirements. Only elders qualify for election to conference leadership and to the bishopric.

In 1977, Bishop Marston wrote a "Life Sketch" in the third person covering significant segments of his life. The section on "His Ministerial Career" beyond local preacher tells how his other steps to the ministry took place:

> He was inclined toward the Christian ministry in his college days but at that time could not sense a definite call. In his sophomore year he was president of the Student Ministerial Association.
>
> He was forced to confront the issue in his mid-thirties while president of Greenville College. Conference action, without his request or consent, made him a member of the conference "on trial." In due course, at the close of the minimum period in this relationship, and still without his request or consent, he was accepted by the conference to full membership and elected to deacon's orders. He now must assume responsibility, for of course, without his consent the bishop could not ordain him. He sought seclusion in which to face the issue, and in prayer was confidently led to accept the action of the conference—and, at the appropriate time, presented himself before George W. Griffith for ordination as deacon.
>
> Ordained deacon, by Bishop George W. Griffith, 1931;
> Ordained elder, by Bishop William Pearce, 1933;
> Elected bishop, by the Board of Administration as the interim authority of the General Conference, 1935.

Responses to Dr. Marston's election ran in two directions. Most telegrams, cards, and letters reflected joy and thanksgiving. Some raised the question of what Greenville College would do without him. A wire the faculty had sent to him in Winona Lake expressed mixed feelings:

"Heartiest congratulations for honor justly conferred, but we simply can't let you go at this critical time with us unless sure that God wills it. Take time for consideration. Think of raising academic standards, the Tower Club, churchwide publicity, North Central Membership—all necessary for our future welfare and growth."

A letter from Mrs. Carl Howland, wife of the editor of the denominational magazine, *The Free Methodist,* took a strong position against his acceptance:

> I feel about your present work the way I feel about Mr. Howland's—it is of greater value and service to the church than the one to which you have been newly elected, and I'd think twice before I gave it up.
>
> As bishop you may have more freedom to write and go to certain places, but it would be confined almost wholly within our church. As a college president you contact the world, colleges, and universities, bringing yourself, our college, and our church to their attention such as you never could as bishop. You are asked to speak before groups as a college president where as a bishop you never would be. . . .
>
> You have brought the standing of the college up where other schools and colleges and universities recognize it because of you. For you to go would change that, for who could take your place? . . .

Bishop Marston responded:

> I appreciate indeed your letter, written I know from your heart. Many others, especially close to Greenville, think as you have written. Poor Lila, *can't* see it any other way. And I recognize the force of what you say—the severing of contacts, and the like. But up to this moment—and I hardly expect the conviction to come now—I have not been able to get my conscience behind a move to resign the election.
>
> Some think I should have an overwhelming conviction to accept and leave Greenville before doing so. In view of my ordination decision—which meant a struggle to me (not of consecration however)—I must have an overpowering conviction to ignore the call of the church. And as time passes, I realize the difficulties of the new position no less, but believe I do recognize aspects of the task that present a real chal-

lenge and of which I am persuaded many are not aware.

But one thing is certain—we can know the will of God, and I have usually discovered that will by proceeding slowly and by faith. I think of other decisions which have been momentous in our lives, and God's guidance therein gives confidence now.

God gave me Isaiah 40:28-31 the evening following the election, not to tell me what to do or relieve the necessity for faith, but to sustain me in the whirl my world was in.

I deeply appreciate your unselfish interest, and trust that I have your confidence that I will do as God wills, as I know the same.

Mrs. Howland's reply showed a willingness to accept God's will and confidence in the new bishop to find and follow God's will. "I believe in God and know He can direct. I have a safe feeling about your desire to know and I am sure you want to and will do the right thing. . . ."

On January 14, 1932, President Marston had written: "Sometimes I still experience my boyhood thrill for the pulpit ministry, but it seems that my ministry is rather the ministry of teaching— and administration."

Now Bishop Marston would have ample opportunity for pulpit ministry. But he would also carry heavy responsibilities in administration. Under this double load, the Scripture he referred to in his letter to Mrs. Howland must have become even more significant to him.

> Hast thou not known? Hast thou not heard, that the everlasting God, the Lord, the Creator of the ends of the earth, fainteth not, neither is weary? There is no searching of his understanding. He giveth power to the faint; and to those that have no might he increaseth strength. Even the youths shall faint and be weary, and the young men shall utterly fall, but they that wait upon the Lord shall renew their strength; they shall mount up with wings like eagles; they shall run, and not be weary; and they shall walk, and not faint.
>
> —Isaiah 40:28-31.

Before the days of electronic wonders and miniaturization, Dr. Marston used a more cumbersome dictating device for his inter-office and business correspondence.

On a world trip, Bishop Marston, an avid photographer,
lay prone in the roadway to get a picture of the Sea of
Galilee (Israel) and flowers along the wayside. One of
his guides holds Marston's hat as a sun-shield for the
camera lens, while another guide also takes a photograph of this strange proceeding. A photographer in
America who processed the photograph commented, "I
never before in my life saw a bishop so low as that!"
Byron S. Lamson, General Missionary Secretary of the
Free Methodist Church, took the picture.

11

Ministry/Family—How to Keep the Balance

In Los Angeles, a former student of the new bishop became concerned. Byron S. Lamson, a Greenville graduate and a man with pastoral experience, was president of Los Angeles Pacific College, a Free Methodist sponsored junior college. He heard murmurings about a bishop who had never pastored a church. President Lamson suggested to the pastor of the college church that they invite Bishop Marston to hold evangelistic meetings for the church and the college. The pastor and his board agreed.

Lamson then went to his college board and suggested they ask the bishop to make a tour of the northern part of the state with him. The board consented. Both the northern tour and the Los Angeles meetings gave Lamson openings to make helpful suggestions to the bishop.

Marston wrote:

> After being with me in the north at Modesto and Santa Cruz, President Lamson said I must break down my messages into series. I say too much in one sermon. I find that is true. . . .
>
> I find that it is important to get the human interest appeal into my messages. Rather reserved and constitutionally introverted, I must strive for this. . . .

Bishop Marston concluded his California trip with the two-week revival meeting at the college church, his first ever, Then, en route from Los Angeles to Greenville, via Santa Fe, he noted in his journal:

> February 24, 1936
>
> President Lamson told me as the meetings neared their close that he had brought me out to help me, but he saw it quite differently before I was through. However, the meetings *did* help me—very valuable experience, and I gained confidence for evangelistic work.
>
> I found the altar appeals especially difficult. And at the close of the first week, on Sunday afternoon, I was at the end of my rope. President Lamson and I prayed earnestly and repeatedly, and my load lifted, and it came to me so forcibly that I should preach the gospel and not strain at the altar call. . . . Thereafter I had greater freedom in the appeal. Although I never stormed the crowds to the altar on a tide of emotion, seekers came deliberately and slowly, perhaps up to fifteen at a service. . . .

The bishop developed strength in preaching that brought results and recognition. He always prepared well and wrote a complete manuscript of his sermons. His style of presentation could be described as lecture form. As he wrote after his California experience, he had to work to include human interest material and not say too much in one sermon. As he succeeded, his sermons caught the minds of his listeners and led them to decisions.*

(A collection of sermons by Bishop Marston, *He Lived on Our Street,* was published posthumously by Light and Life Press, 1979.)

Before 1936 ended, Bishop Marston put into practice what he had learned about improving his preaching. He accepted most requests to hold revival meetings. He saw lives changed as people responded to invitations to accept Christ. But his tendency to overwork undermined his once robust strength. These excerpts from his letters to Lila tell the story:

---

*Because of the strength of Bishop Marston's sermonic material and his use of manuscripts, his sermons attracted the attention of men like Dr. Andrew Blackwood, professor of homiletics at Princeton. Dr. Blackwood included sermons from Bishop Marston in two of his books. For *Evangelical Sermons of Our Day* (1959) Marston contributed, "The Hunger of the Soul." *Special Day Sermons for Evangelicals* (1961) included his sermon, "When Jesus Comes to Our Town."

November 2, 1936
Lockport, New York

How crowded I have been! I preached Friday evening, spoke three times Saturday, traveled by train nearly three hundred miles, arrived at Lockport near two in the morning. Without my usual margin of reserve energy, it has been hard. Such fatigue, with aching limbs and old-age decrepitude. I know you would excuse my failure to write yesterday if you knew how I have been driven. I am on the upgrade, and now the big crush is over for this week. Excepting my evening services, I have only two radio messages and one more high school assembly. I have Saturday night off, too.

Early this morning I went to the big high school and addressed the superior group, eight or ten hundred. The principal was very "skittish" indeed, fearing that I would engage in a sectarian tirade. You recall the telegram asking for my subject—well, he wanted to know as a safeguard, and when I wired in reply, "Where Do You Live?" he was not much enlightened. He was nervous, but I didn't allow his fright to tie me up. I had a splendid time for twenty-five minutes challenging that bright group of young people to high living. As soon as I sat down, the principal commended me highly and told me how absorbed in my message every youngster was. And what a hand they gave me!

November 4, 1936
Lockport, New York
My dear Lila,

I got up at five this morning to go into Buffalo for a broadcast at 8:05. It seems that I got across in good shape. My voice is suited to radio. I gave a cutting from my book, *From Chaos to Character,* on the Christian way as not cramped and narrow, and yet a way of trial. For God's purpose with man is not to indulge him but to restore in him God's image. Tomorrow morning I plan something less heavy, probably character studies of Andrew and Philip.

Can you not feel that you have a part in this work I am doing—by being loyal and brave, and by your prayers? Prompt the little ones to pray for Daddy in his work, as well as for his personal welfare.

November 6, 1936
Lockport, New York
My dear little family,

I am still far from well. I get little sleep, but that doesn't seem to be a great hardship. Last night I slept until four o'clock, then read until six-thirty, then slept until nine. Such pain and discomfort!

I feel better today, but there is little evidence that I am shaking off the neuritis. As a life malady it isn't so pleasant. . . . I am trusting the Lord to help me overcome the disease. . . .

My typewriter is a great help. It occurs to me that you ought to have a household mangle for your ironing to balance this typewriter as a labor-saving tool for me. Why not ask Illinois Power and Light to leave you one for a week's demonstration? Seriously now, I urge it . . . one that will handle shirts and everything you iron with much less time and effort.

I think I am improving in preaching ability and ease—and I love the work! It is a wonderful challenge to face a congregation night after night with the opportunity of building a structure of truth that will influence men for eternity. Please, darling Lila, can't you get inspiration for this new work?

November 7, 1936
Lockport, New York

Have been in much pain today. The neuritis seems to have a very firm grip. I cannot stay in one position so sitting and lying are very painful.

We had a very big crowd last night—quite remarkable! I made one of my very best addresses on "Prodigal Parents," and the audience appreciated it. I will try to send you the newspaper announcement. We get very good publicity here.

November 10, 1936
Conneaut, Ohio
Dearest Lila,

I went to Lockport's leading physician yesterday morning before I left. I had slept well all night Sunday night. The doctor gave me a pretty thorough checkup. . . . He said to me, "You have been going at a pretty fast pace, haven't you?" I told him I had had a hard summer. . . . He says I must get rest, and that my trouble is with my nerves—not sciatica, lumbago, etc. The trouble has seized me just now in the region of the sciatic nerve, but the fact that my difficulties roam about the body, striking now here and now there, indicates nerve exhaustion.

Medication and some moderation of schedule helped. But Bishop Marston continued to pour himself into his work. His compulsion drove him. This was a part of his introverted temperament. He wanted to do everything, and he wanted to do it with perfection. Success gave him needed reinforcement, but his double concerns for success and humility stretched him almost to the breaking point.

When Bishop Marston held a meeting in a church, it spilled over into the community. He was invited to speak at a series of union services in Pennsylvania in January 1938. This community event was called "Teaching Mission on Some Essentials of Christian Faith and Practice." From letters home, his feelings concerning this endeavor are seen:

January 10, 1938

Last night the first union service was held at the Baptist Church. It was full, with several extra chairs. A fine old structure, very worshipful. But I made a mistake—leaving my frock coat at home. This town, though smaller than Greenville, is more conservative. All the other preachers were there in regulation garb. But I didn't let my short-tail confound me, and for a union service in a strange place, had great liberty. The service was an excellent beginning. The preachers of the town are very fine to me, and the townspeople likewise. Last week union prayer services were held in preparation for this week. . . .

January 11

Notwithstanding the weather and that it was Monday night, we had a large attendance last night, the church auditorium being comfortably full with a few in the balcony. Again I had a good time preaching, declaring strong truth concerning the way of salvation. I believe that the most critical of our people will admit that I did not "pull my punch" because of the other churches and their ministers. There are few communities where the preachers so unanimously would endorse such truth. . . .

Give Bobby my special love on his birthday. I am so sorry that I cannot help him celebrate. Tell him that I'm depending on him to make things go aright while I am away. "We men folks must stand together."

January 13

It was the night after my third message that the group opened wide their arms with no reservations, but with un-qualified endorsement. The two preceding nights they ac-cepted my message and were moved by it, but Tuesday night they accepted me. . . . It is a wonderful sight—the mul-titudes crowding out on these snowy nights to hear the gos-pel. Our people are enthusiastic, with no critics. It is agreed by all of them that I am not compromising the truth. I am convinced that our people limit our usefulness by drawing a wall around them, and then declaring that the other churches will have nothing to do with us. . . .

January 14

Your two letters and the package came last evening. Thanks so much for taking care of the matter so well. The coat was so well packed it doesn't need pressing. How did you do it? . . .

January 17

Saturday evening I had unusual freedom in preaching with an altar service. . . . It is estimated that my audience num-bered 800 last night—but let's be conservative and say 750. Again I was swung out of myself and did some good preaching with the Lord's help. You know me well enough to understand that God was there, or I would have been stiff and stilted. The Lord has been with me in every service but one—the first one at the Presbyterian Church just after the great popularity wave swept over me, and I became frightened lest I get into bondage, and got into bondage to my fright of bondage. . . .

Bishop Marston's administrative correspondence files contain letters marked, "Not sent." He suppressed his introversion and wrote boldly. But when he read the letters, he thought they were too strong. Others were sent but followed the next day with a letter of apology for his harshness.

A personal letter to his daughter, Evelyn, shows his tenderness as he asked for her forgiveness:

> October 6, 1938
> Centralia, Illinois
> Dear Evelyn:
>
> I must ask your forgiveness again. This noon at lunch, while you *were* wrong in what you said, I was too harsh and quick to punish you. I should have controlled myself better, but under the pressure of my mistake this morning and my haste to get off to Centralia, I didn't use good judgment. I have felt so bad about it. I wanted to drive home tonight to see you, but Mother thinks I shouldn't. But I want to feel right, and so write you this letter. Will you forgive me?

The intensity of the bishop's schedule made problems for his family. His letters to Lila reflect the loneliness expressed in her letters. He adjusted his schedule some.

But he found ways to compensate for those extended absences. In the summer when school was out, he took the family with him. Canada, California—and nearly every state in the Union—were on the itinerary at one time or another. Evelyn recalls those long family automobile trips—sometimes *all* summer—as highlights of her childhood. She writes:

> Daddy would always find the most scenic or historic route between the locations of his summer appointments. We visited most of the national parks and often rented a cabin for a day or two. Perhaps it was fishing in Yellowstone (where Bobby got lost on one such trip) that gave both Bob and me our love for fishing even today. We carried in our luggage (and there was lots of it) a small camping mess kit and Mother learned to fry that fish to perfection. She even enjoyed catching it, too.
>
> In the winter during Dad's periods at home, he would plan time to spend with Bob and me, making picture maps in our basement recreation room. Using picture postcards and our

own snapshots we would fashion large maps of the national parks and historic areas visited the summer before.

Another warm memory of Daddy's times at home is of our weekly "family night." I remember the fireplace and popcorn, silly skits Bobby and I worked up, home movie nights when we enjoyed reliving our trips by viewing the 16mm movies Dad had taken, reading and playing games together.

Bob, who is now a pastor in Michigan, when asked if he felt shortchanged by having a part-time father, said:

> I didn't at the time. I didn't realize the sacrifices he was making or the sacrifices Mother was making or the sacrifices I in turn was making. But looking back, I realize that it was a difficult thing. It meant a lot of time away from home for Dad—more time than it does today for executives perhaps because of the air travel now. He was home twenty to twenty-five percent of the time.
>
> We traveled with Dad in the summertime. A day off for him might mean driving 700 miles to get to a destination. But we kept the speed limit. Dad wouldn't break it.
>
> When I was quite young, I'd go upstairs to Dad's study and lie on the floor and wait for Dad to have some time for me. He had bushels of mail waiting for him when he came home, and bushels to get out. He didn't have time to relax and rest and work around the house. There was the pressure of that mail. I'd stay there on the floor, play with a toy car, and wait for him to get the mail ready for me to take to the post office. At about ten minutes to five, I'd run the mail down. When I got back, we'd go out and play catch. When he was able to spend time with me, he gave me quality time.

Bishop Marston, in looking back on those years, wrote about an event which he called "A Profitable Investment":

> A minister in another state had requested my services in a Sunday-to-Sunday preaching mission, but I was impressed that I should insist upon a Monday-to-Sunday commitment. Although I had no clear reason for refusing the initial Sunday, later developments were to reveal the leading of Providence in the final arrangement.

During the two weeks at home, I began with Bobby the building of a toy boat, to be driven by a large rubber band under tension. The boy's interest in the project was keen, and afternoons he would hurry home from school and call to me in my upstairs study, "Daddy, are we going to work on the boat today?" And I would lay aside whatever task was then engaging me to go with the lad to the furnace room "to work on the boat."

The stern-wheeler finally was completed. Launched in a farmyard pond, it bravely plied its way on the water under its own power—the pride and joy of its builders.

The evening of March 8, 1942, came—the Sunday I had refused to give to the Michigan pastor. At the home church that evening was the concluding service of an evangelistic series. The speaker was a great favorite of Bobby's crowd. During the invitation hymn, Bobby stood between his father and mother. I was impressed to speak a word to Bobby about yielding his life to Jesus Christ.

Knowing the lad's sensitiveness to parental attention in public, I quietly seated myself at Bobby's side, thus inconspicuously bringing my voice near the lad's ear. A few whispered words from his daddy, a few moments of troubled hesitation on Bobby's part—and suddenly and resolutely he pressed his way to the aisle of the crowded church and proceeded to the altar of prayer. Other boys of Bobby's crowd soon followed.

He is Pastor Bob now. On this Father's Day of 1970, looking backward over a long life, I consider the time I spent building a toy boat with a nine-year-old son one of my most profitable investments.

Son Bob Marston waits for his father to complete the day's mail so they can have time to do things together.

Family togetherness was enjoyed in the deep woods. Bob, Lila, and Evelyn often traveled with Bishop Marston on his long trips between appointments.

Wide-eyed wonderment is a natural result of exploring the mysteries of a flowing creek.

Bob, Evelyn, and Lila gaze out across a lake high in the Colorado Rockies.

Like father, like son— fishing runs in the family. They all enjoyed eating what they could catch.

One of the hobbies of Bishop Marston was making illustrated maps using picture postcards and snapshots from their summer trips. This was a wintertime family project in the basement of their home.

Marston family devotions by fireside.

12

Measuring Up to Myriad Demands

Several major ministries, demanding in themselves, only partially represent the full load Bishop Marston carried. Administration was always upon him. He shared with the other three bishops the supervision of the conferences. This included conducting from six to eleven annual conferences of two to seven days each summer, visiting the conferences during the year, and handling problems that surfaced. All of this demanded much in personal sacrifice by the bishop and his family.

Early in this period of Bishop Marston's life he completed his third book, *Youth Speaks!** Material was collected in classroom situations, as he explained in the foreword:

> The core of the book is made up of youth's own record of its problems. Over a period of a decade the writer collected from junior and senior college students in psychology, mental hygiene, and related subjects, written memories of their teen-age problems and experiences. These records were submitted anonymously, and further to insure complete frankness the instructor promised not to read the records within a year of their writing. Students thus had full assurance that the instructor could not identify writer and record.

---

*Marston, L. R., *Youth Speaks!,* Light and Life Press, 1939. First-person accounts of problems of college juniors and seniors, including Marston's interpretations and suggested solutions. The book was planned for and used largely by nonprofessional parents, church school leaders, as well as by pastors.

Eight chapters quoted extensively from the teen-age memoirs and interpreted them. The last three chapters traced ". . . the direction of recent trends of thought and morals bearing upon youth, and point the way out of the present confusion through a new recognition of moral freedom and a realistic accounting of sin. . . ."

Vigorous Leadership Strengthens Church

The Free Methodist Church has four commissions in its general organization: Administration, Christian Education, Evangelism, and Missions. Because Bishop Marston was elected to replace the late Bishop Zahniser, he took leadership of the Commission on Evangelism which Zahniser formerly headed. His leadership in evangelism proved advantageous. With his skills as a leader and his concern for persons, he brought renewed aggressiveness to soul winning. He developed tests and tools to help pastors. He urged the church to have a better image of itself. He insisted on singing an old hymn as an affirmation rather than a question: "Thy grace *is* as mighty now as when Elijah felt its power."

Bishop Marston became chairman of the Commission on Christian Education in 1939. During the next eight years he led in the development of policies and programs that enhanced the total Christian Education ministry of the church.*

The responsibility of the Commission reached from Sunday school to colleges. During Marston's administration this expanded to seminary, lay training programs, servicemen, and the expansion of ministries to children and youth.

Seminary Is Established

His interest in a seminary for Free Methodist ministerial students predated Marston's service as chairman of the Commission on Christian Education. In fact, when asked what led to thinking about starting a seminary, Marston referred to his days as president of Greenville when he had worked with Biblical Seminary in New York [interdenominational] for the training of Greenville graduates. At that time interest developed for a Free Methodist seminary.

---

*Bishop Marston received an honorary LL.D degree in 1939, conferred by Houghton College. In 1942, Greenville College conferred on him an honorary D.D. degree.

When he became chairman of the Commission on Christian Education, Bishop Marston led in finding an answer to the need. The interest grew. In 1944, under the recommendations from the trustees of our leading colleges, supported by the Association of Colleges, and with requests from the students themselves, the Commission on Christian Education recommended to the Board of Administration the setting up of planning committees looking toward the opening of a seminary in the fall of 1946. The Board approved.

The following spring (1945) the committees, together with the Commission, prepared the tentative outline of the project. The Executive Commission received their report and asked Bishop Marston, as chairman of the Commission on Christian Education, to survey superintendents and representative pastors to determine their attitude toward partial support of the proposed seminary. Nearly 80 percent thought a seminary should be provided as soon as possible.

Upon action of the Board of Administration, John Wesley Seminary was organized November 1, 1945, with plans to open in September 1947. Bishop Marston was elected chairman of the executive board of the seminary.

But difficulties were encountered in securing a campus. No definite financial provision had been made. What about a library, staff, accreditation? Before the new venture could get under way, another option appeared.

Asbury Theological Seminary, located in Wilmore, Kentucky, is an accredited, independent institution in the Methodist tradition. If the church could affiliate its theological training program with an existing seminary, it could provide immediate accredited training for its young men and women. In the spring of 1946, George Turner, a Free Methodist professor at Asbury, suggested such an affiliation with his institution. In August 1946, the Executive Board of John Wesley Seminary decided to associate with Asbury for a three-year trial period. This affiliation worked so much to the advantage of both institutions that it still continues as John Wesley Seminary Foundation.*

Immediately upon the Board's approval of John Wesley Seminary, Bishop Marston began his search for significant books for the library. Many valuable volumes were secured.

---

*A similar arrangement has been in effect with Western Evangelical Seminary in Portland, Oregon, since 1975.

As early as 1947, Bishop Marston was elected a member of the Board of Trustees of Asbury Theological Seminary. He continued in that responsibility until 1974, ten years beyond his retirement as bishop. At that time Asbury made him a "Life Trustee," expressing on a printed document, ". . . thanks to Almighty God for Bishop Marston's long and dedicated life and ministry and heartfelt appreciation for his many years of influential service on this Board of Trustees."

Church Laity Receives Study Helps

Under Bishop Marston's leadership, the Commission on Christian Education also developed a program of helps for the laity of the church. The lay training program did not involve the extensive efforts required for the seminary. But Christian Service Training, under the directorship of Dr. Orville S. Walters, made a significant contribution to the spiritual life of the church. Dr. Walters developed a curriculum for personal and group study that helps young Christians understand the Bible and its application to practical Christian living and service. It ministers to more mature Christians by helping them grow spiritually and in leadership ability.

The Imperative of World War II

In St. Petersburg, Florida, for an eight-day meeting, Bishop Marston awakened December 7, 1941 from a Sunday afternoon nap to hear the shrill radio announcement that the Japanese had attacked Pearl Harbor. The United States was instantly embroiled in a global conflict. The following summer Marston wrote, "It seemed a dream—but such folly for them to attack such a nation as the U.S. We didn't know their strength."

The Commission on Christian Education faced two new challenges because of the war: facilitating entrance into the chaplaincy by pastors, and ministering to the church's men in service. The first posed a special problem. Bishop Marston explained it in a statement issued November 4, 1942:

> The Free Methodist Church as a small denomination does not have a quota of chaplains assigned to it [by the government]. Although our men in the Armed Forces run into thousands, not enough of them are stationed at one place or

on a single ship to provide a congregation. Other small churches are likewise denied a quota.

The Free Methodist Church, however, has established an affiliation with the Methodist Commission on Chaplains under which approved Free Methodist candidates are considered for endorsement by the Methodist Commission under the Methodist quota.

The arrangement was first suggested by the United States General Commission on Army and Navy Chaplains. It worked well. Because the Methodist Church could not fill its quota, openings were available for Free Methodist pastors. Once given ecclesiastical endorsement by their own church, they were processed in a routine manner. They found a rich ministry to the servicemen of many churches and those with no church. Similar arrangements helped Canadian pastors enter the chaplaincy. This procedure, developed by Marston, is still in effect.

The Church Council for Men in Service was formed in July 1942 to minister to both the United States' and Canada's men and women in military service. The first office was in Marston's basement recreation room. A letter Bishop Marston wrote to parents of men and women in service told about the ministry:

December 25, 1943
Dear Friend of the "Blue Star" Fellowship:

Your home circle has been broken by our country's call, and this year your Christmas joy has an undertone of sadness because of the vacant chair, the empty room, the quiet house.

We who are endeavoring in the name of the Church and its Christ to bring cheer to those in our Armed Forces do not forget you who must "keep the home fires burning" until their return. At this Christmas season, may you catch a new vision, even through your tears and because of your heartache, of that love of God so great that He gave us His Son on the first Christmas so long ago.

You may know that the Church Council has been sending Christian literature and encouraging letters to the thousands in our servicemen's fellowship, and when possible has kept our Service Pastors across the nation in touch with them. From their own letters of gratitude, we are led to believe that we have in a measure been successful in bringing to them courage for dark days. . . .

As our Christmas greetings to the thousands on our service roster, Mr. Brandt has just mailed an attractive little devotional booklet entitled, "Look and Live." . . . Each week he sends birthday greetings to those whose birthdays are approaching and record of which is on file here in the office.

We desire that you know of our interest in your "Blue Star" hero and in you. Write us if in any way we can assist you or yours during this period of stress. God grant that our boys may soon be home again, sound in body and strong in spirit! And although this for you may not be a "Merry Christmas," may it be a "Blessed Christmas" because you cast all your care on Him who cares for you.

An Adventure to Write Home About!

Alert to the excitement of all of life, Bishop Marston made the most of every situation—even enjoying what might have been a harrowing experience. Of such a time in March 1943, he wrote a letter to his family:

> 2:45 p.m.—snowbound on the
> only narrow-gauge passenger
> train in the United States.
> Dear Lila,
>
> Here's a letter to keep. Four hours ago our train bucked a big snowdrift—for a blizzard is on—and came to a rather quick stop. A four-driver, low-wheeled engine built for power over this mountain, with a mail car, baggage car, two coaches, and a parlor-dinette combination. We are between four and five miles from the continental divide.
>
> Now the snow is drifting . . . and the window where I sit is drifted more than halfway to the top. [Trainmen] have telephoned our condition to the dispatcher, and a rotary snowplow is being sent to our rescue. Probably will not reach us before dark, and we will do well to reach Durango [Colorado] for breakfast tomorrow. The rotary will come up grade behind us, back to a switch a mile or two below us, send an engine up to hook on to our rear to pull us out. But the snow is drifting in around us. . . .

I pulled some old socks on over my shoes, tucked trouser legs in them, walked up the train as far as I could through the baggage car, then outside, fighting my way to the engine, and took movies! Then went in the cab with the engineer and got warm—aplenty! Trouser legs were not even wet, shoes dry when I got back.

About two miles back on a curve, the train had stopped to get up a good head of steam for bucking drifts—and I was able to get a picture of the engine from a vestibule door. I took it, thinking we might get stuck, and I would want "scene 2." In fact, when we struck the big drift that stalled us, I was almost conscience-stricken for having hoped—I couldn't help it—that we would be hung up for an hour perhaps—just for the experience and the picture!

Don't forget to read this to Bobby. Tell him it reminds me of the adventures of Huck Finn, and I wish he (Bobby) were with me. . . .

Can you imagine such country as we are in? I am enjoying the experience—but don't want too much of it. But anyway, if you get this you'll know I am safe in Durango.

Participants in the official convocation of John Wesley Seminary Foundation at Wilmore, Kentucky, February 23 and 24, 1948: Bishops Marston, Ormston, and Taylor, and Dr. W. C. Mavis, dean of the Foundation.

In the early 1940s, Marston initiated the Church Council for Men in Service to assist personnel in the armed forces. The first office was set up in the basement of Marston's home in Greenville, Illinois. Shown with Bishop Marston is M. E. Brandt, executive secretary.

13

Marston and the National Association of Evangelicals

It started in New England.

There a fellowship was formed in 1929 as ". . . a united front for evangelicals and as a means of cooperation among them in various spiritual objectives." The New England Fellowship conferences of 1939, 1940, and 1941, adopted resolutions calling for a national movement which resulted in a meeting of leaders in Chicago, October 1941. Looking back, Bishop Marston outlined the sequence of events:

> At the Chicago meeting it was unanimously decided that the next step should be a call for a national conference of evangelicals, including leaders of various denominations, mission boards, colleges, seminaries, institutes, the religious press, and interdenominational organizations at which all suggestions and plans might be received and considered. . . .

A temporary committee headed by J. Elwin Wright, Executive Secretary of the NEF, issued the call for the meeting in St. Louis. Bishop Marston accepted the invitation to attend. Marston continued his story:

> I was present at the historic St. Louis Conference of April 1942, and witnessed the formulation of a remarkable Christian Fellowship, embracing representatives of a wide variety of Christian organizations and denominations. These found

common ground as together they faced Christ as the center and sought in Him the essentials of evangelical faith.

As the meeting closed, Marston was elected second vice president of the fledgling organization which named itself the National Association of Evangelicals. Dr. Harold John Ockenga, pastor of Park Street Church in Boston, became the first president. The delegates called for a Constitutional Convention for 1943.

Bishop Marston recorded his reactions:

> It was my privilege to work with the executive committee during this first and formative year, leading up to the Constitutional Convention of April 1943 in Chicago. How carefully and prayerfully that committee proceeded, again and again sensing the uplift and direction of a power and wisdom not our own. During these months there came a growing realization that the movement was greater than its human leadership, and that those directing its affairs were indeed led, and on occasion, overruled by His Spirit.
>
> Some wondered when would come the disillusionment of selfish bickering and bigoted dissension which have disrupted so many efforts of ardent believers to find a common ground for Christian action. The year approached its close with the Constitutional Convention looming before us. Could we adopt a constitution and a working policy as harmoniously as the preliminary organization had been effected and to this point maintained? Or would the convention wreck the movement?

Bishop Marston was elected first vice president at the Constitutional Convention in Chicago.

One year later at the Columbus convention, he was elected president. But it did not happen without incident. A vocal minority in the movement thought NAE should focus its efforts on direct attacks on the Federal (now National) Council of Churches (FCC). This included separation from any denomination affiliated with the Council. Marston, with the majority, believed that since NAE was not a church nor a council of churches, but a fellowship and service organization, the restrictions should not apply. Membership should be based on the acceptance of the Statement of Faith.*

---

*Appendix III gives NAE Statement of Faith.

Threats of withdrawal from NAE by the vocal minority intimidated many delegates. But not Marston. He wrote to Dr. R. L. Decker of Kansas City, who was elected first vice president but had to leave the convention early.

> April 15, 1944
> Dear Dr. Decker:
> A brief report. Shortly after you left me last night relief came to me, and guided me. One brother, either before or after you left, said he felt he must withdraw from the movement if that clause to which I objected were not included. I answered that before the vote was taken I desired to make clear my position, which I would maintain regardless of the vote, for I would not seem to resort to a threat. It had become clear to me that with such a difference between us [myself and the vocal minority], another would make a more effective president, and I insisted that my name be removed from candidacy for the presidency. . . . I believed that God was in the movement and would continue with it. However, I could not as president give such whole-souled support as a president must give: that as vice president I could work for the cause and leave defense of the organization at certain points of personal disagreement to others. As an individual and as vice president I could accept the restrictive clause, but as president I could not.
> This was a block-buster! It was approaching 4:00 a.m., or probably past 3:00, when we adjourned.

Marston was elected president of NAE. The bishop's tenacity paid off, and both he and the organization gained by it. To Lila, he wrote concerning his acceptance of the presidency:

> I can't do other than accept—my every demand has been met. The crowd has rallied solidly—no schism with any, but even those whose policies I questioned are emphatically with me as a policy of moderation. The Lord has undertaken in a marvelous way: such Christian love, such loyalty, such men of God! I couldn't refuse in the end.
> There will be frequent trips to New York, Boston, etc. That is my church territory next year, you see! Also, I'll expect to fly quite a little to save time.

Already $35,000 has been raised! This is wonderful. I didn't want the job—and God in a marvelous way ironed out all wrinkles and gave me a steady assurance that He had charge. It reminds me of my leaving Greenville in 1926 and going to Washington. Shrinking, holding back, and then venturing out confidently by faith.

God has given me this—this morning when nothing was settled and I nevertheless was calm and yielded:

"But I will tarry at Ephesus until Pentecost. For a great door and effectual is opened unto me, and there are many adversaries" (I Corinthians 16:8, 9).

Lila dear—your part in this may be the hard one again. But you have a part—don't worry, leave things with God. Rejoice that I have before me this great door, and stand by me when I must fight the many adversaries.

Love,
Leslie

P.S. Again as with the Washington move and the bishop's move, I have a calm confidence that this is the call of destiny, and I dare not ignore it.

The step was so against my selfish desires and interests that I have been protected at that point.

Bishop Marston gave NAE strong leadership as president during his two-year term and beyond in other capacities. He helped organize World Relief and headed it from 1950 to 1959. He was involved in the organization of the National Sunday School Association. He served as a member of the Commission on a Christian Philosophy of Education. Mrs. Marston helped organize the Women's Fellowship of NAE and served as president from 1948-1951.

On May 22, 1944, Dr. Ockenga wrote:

My dear Bishop Marston:

For some time since being involved in the National Association of Evangelicals, I have felt the need of a small group of evangelical leaders gathering for a thorough discussion of the underlying apologetic of the evangelical movement in America. I am convinced that if any evangelical movement is to succeed, it must be on a firm basis.

With the thought of gathering together ten or a dozen

professors and leaders for a week's discussion, I approached a friend of mine with the idea.

He, in turn, has turned over to me his beautiful summer home which is adequate to accommodate twelve of us for a week's time, and he has agreed to pay all expenses to bring a dozen men whom I will select to Massachusetts, and to return them to their homes.

After the date and personnel of the conference are decided, I will divide up certain topics, probably dealing with Theism, with revelation, with the possibility in believing in the substitutionary satisfaction of Christ, and with the Church, so that the days may be directed by different leaders.

Let me repeat that it will cost you nothing to come to this conference from the moment you leave your home until the moment you return. All I ask is a willingness to reevaluate the bases of our evangelical faith. Please let me hear from you as soon as possible.

With best wishes, I am

> Faithfully yours,
> H. J. Ockenga

Bishop Marston participated in the conference and at another in 1945. From the second conference he wrote to Lila:

Monday evening, August 28

What a day! Again a wonderful time, and tremendously important to me intellectually and doctrinally. I think I am getting to the very heart of the distinction between Calvinism and Wesleyanism.* I am the only Wesleyan here, and it is fortunate at least one is here. But wonderful fellowship!

Swimming today. You should have seen me astride Ockenga's shoulders fighting young Woods on our host's shoulders. We downed them.

The beach is wonderful. One can go far out. We don't get the big waves because we are protected by Cape Cod's long arm, elbow bent.

---

*In an illustrated lecture entitled "The Continental Divide in Christian Doctrine," Marston gave a graphic portrayal of the contrast between God's justice as represented by Calvinism and God's love as represented by Wesleyan Arminianism. He showed that God's love and His justice meet in His holiness at the cross. See Appendix IV.

A strong friendship developed between the bishop and Dr. Ockenga. Many years later Dr. Ockenga said of him:

> As I look back over the 30 years or more that our fellowship and activity in the NAE lasted, I must confess that I leaned upon Leslie Marston as on few others. I valued his wisdom, his commitment to the evangelical cause, and his fidelity, and counted them as pillars upon which we could build. Men of his calibre made the NAE. . . .
>
> An incident which impresses itself upon me was at the scholars' conferences which I called at Manomet Point in Massachusetts for two summers. We were talking as we walked along the beach about men whom God was using. We each contributed several recollections of such men, as we knew them in that day.
>
> As I look back upon him, I think of a strong leader with deep convictions, of personal humility, and one who always placed others before himself. I would have felt that he would have made a fine first president of the NAE instead of myself. He always supported me in every detail of our work.

Bishop Marston addressing a convention of the National Association of Evangelicals in Chicago.

Billy Graham, George Ford (then executive secretary of NAE) and L. R. Marston confer at the 1956 convention.

Bishop Marston with other NAE officer at the national convention in Denver, 1966.

The Protestant Voice, announcing Bishop Marston's election as president of the National Association of Evangelicals in 1944, also published this cartoon and then sent the artist's original to him. The drawing features some of the bishop's past fields of activity.

14

Horizons Continue
to Widen

The *Town Meeting of the Air,* in its 20th year of broadcasting on the ABC radio network, invited Dr. Marston to participate in a discussion for June 22, 1954. The program centered on "American Family Life: Chaos or Character?" Drawn so directly from Marston's book, *From Chaos to Character,* he was familiar with the subject.

The real significance of this event, however, was its demonstration of Marston's ever widening horizon of influence. Since his capacity always exceeded his job, outside opportunities came to him.

Dr. Alfred Baldwin, Professor and Chairman, Department of Child Development and Family Relationships of Cornell University, joined Dr. Marston on the program.

Marston spoke first. He stated: ". . . many families are building character; others are breeding chaos. . . ." He pointed out that while frequency of divorce was then approaching the level ". . . reached in the decaying Roman Empire in the third century, neither divorce nor delinquency causes family breakdown. They are, rather, symptoms of the decay of the family." He defined the cause of the problem as ". . . selfishness and unrestrained desire for personal pleasure."

He continued with his landmark opening statement:

It is my conviction that strong and stable personalities must be molded, and that to accomplish this end, patterns of right living are essential. It is our claim that the parent or the society that indulges children without responsibility contributes to one of the following results: either youth who break society through delinquency; or youth who are broken in personality through frustration because life has neither goals nor the direction of stable standards; youth who react to license and indulgence with revolutionary idealism, seeking to overthrow society to establish some new order.

Chaos threatens the American family and America. But chaos is not inevitable if the integrating forces of moral responsibility and religious faith are directed to the building of personal, family, and national character.

Dr. Baldwin agreed with Dr. Marston regarding the problems facing America. But he did not accept the assertion that the family was the primary cause. He said, ". . . the cure for our present ills is not a return to family life of the last century. . . . Anything we propose in the way of a remedy at the present time is hardly more than a guess. We do not know enough about personality and the way it develops to have any sound basis for action. . . . Let us strongly support research to discover the relation of family life to our national character so that our proposals for action may in the future stem from a sound foundation of knowledge."

With the issue defined and their positions made clear, the two men continued the discussion between themselves, with the moderator, and in response to questions from the audience. Marston stood for ethical values, inculcated through the family and undergirded by Bible reading and prayer. Baldwin held to the pragmatic approach, emphasizing that what works is right. He did leave some room for ethics but wanted it separated from religion.

Seventeen years after the publication of his book, Marston's recognition as an authority on family life and child development continued, in spite of changes in occupation and the passing of time. He did not lose his expanding vision of God's work in the world and his part in it. He demonstrated the truth of Proverbs 4:18:

> "The path of the righteous is like the first gleam of dawn,
> shining ever brighter till the full light of day." (NIV)

Harmony in Action

Dr. Marston became the senior bishop of the Free Methodist Church in 1947. In this capacity he was the leader of the leaders and chairman of the Board of Administration. For eleven years, from 1947 to 1958, four men served together as bishops. They were:

	Term	Years in Office	Affectionately known to each other
L. R. Marston	1935-1964	29	"Pop" (Senior)
M. D. Ormston	1936-1958	22	"Doc" (M.D.)
C. V. Fairbairn	1939-1961	22	"Chuck"
J. P. Taylor	1947-1964	17	"Jess"

Of this unbroken episcopal team for eleven years, Bishop Marston said, "Four men unlike in personality, temperament and gifts: they worked together without friction, each with high esteem and deep affection for his three comrades."

Florence Taylor, who was secretary to Bishop Marston and now is administrative assistant to the Board of Bishops, wrote her appraisal of him:

> Leslie R. Marston certainly was endowed with the gift of administration. I realize now that his expertise as a presiding officer made it possible for me as a novice minutes-taker, with no training and little instruction, to feel at ease and gain some confidence in a very frightening task.
>
> He had insight that few persons have exhibited. He knew parliamentary law so that his guidance of discussion brought order out of possible chaos of motions, substitute motions, and amendments.
>
> And to warm any secretary's heart, he always stated concisely and clearly the motion being considered.
>
> Coupled with these abilities, he was a man of principle, conviction, and strength. Thus he was able to see a clear path and guide the discussions through the maze that seemed to fog others' minds.
>
> Another important quality of Bishop Marston's was that of kindness/consideration. The heat of debate or difficult personnel matters did not make him insensitive to others' feelings and perspectives.

Preserving the Heritage

When a long-time friend was recuperating in the hospital from serious surgery, Bishop Marston wrote to him and to his wife Esther:

Dr. and Mrs. George L. Ford
Room 5414
St. Luke's Hospital
St. Louis, Missouri

Christmas-tide 1970

Dear friends:

How we rejoice with multitudes in your splendid progress! The Lord grant the progress may continue to full recovery, and speedily.

This has been an ordeal for both of you; the Lord has sustained. Again, I recall my own crisis of fifteen years ago this very month—the surgeon was generous and released me a day or so early that I might be home for Christmas.

It was a fresh, new world! The blessings I had taken for granted before, now became *so real*—and I purposed that never again would I take for granted the mercies of the Lord.

Before my crisis, I had hesitated, and then quite definitely declined the request of my fellow bishops to write the church's history. While still in the hospital after the operation [removal of a malignant kidney], with the encouragement of Mrs. Marston and Z. E. Kellum (my hospital "pastor"), the task challenged me; and it seemed in a sense a special call. To accomplish this, I had been delivered from disease and was on my way to recovery. That task was completed more than ten years ago—and still I am here with the challenge of further tasks.

Yours in Him,
L. R. and Lila Marston

From Age to Age a Living Witness (Winona Lake, Indiana, Light and Life Press, 1960), the six-hundred page historical interpretation of Free Methodism's first century, amounted to more than Bishop Marston first intended. He explained in the preface that he originally planned to write the history of the church from 1915 where Bishop Wilson T. Hogue's two-volume work ended. But typical of Leslie Marston, he decided to do a thorough job and lay a firm foundation.

He began with John Wesley's quest, his Aldersgate experience and beyond, the roots of the Methodist movement, and the message and results of Methodism's witness in eighteenth century England.

He then described Methodism's spread to America and subsequently, the blurring of its witness in doctrine, life and social issues in the mid-nineteenth century. In the chapter "The Lord Sent a Prophet," the reader is introduced to Benjamin Titus Roberts, a pastor in the Methodist Episcopal Church and later the principal founder of the Free Methodist Church. The stresses in the Methodist Episcopal Church between leaders and the reformers, which led to the founding of the Free Methodist Church in 1860, are fully detailed. Then follows the extensive account of the witness maintained and extended through the first one hundred years of the new Methodist denomination.

Summarized here are statements concerning the issues of Free Methodism's origin as given in the section "The Witness Maintained."*

1. *Doctrine:* The Scriptural doctrine of entire sanctification according to the Arminian-Wesleyan interpretation;

2. *Experience:* A corresponding experience of cleansing and power;

3. *Worship:* Spirituality and simplicity of worship in the freedom of the Spirit;

4. *Piety:* A way of holy living that separates the Christian from the world;

5. *Stewardship:* Full consecration for service to God and man.

Bishop Marston's life-long interest in and study of John Wesley and B. T. Roberts, along with extensive and scholarly research, produced a well documented but readable volume. The work brought him recognition as the official church historian and the preserver of the heritage of the denomination.**

---

*From Age to Age a Living Witness, p. 252.

**Donald E. Baker, an editor of Indiana University's *Indiana Magazine of History* wrote, "*From Age to Age a Living Witness* . . . seems based on sounder scholarship and a broader outlook than are many denominational histories."

World Fellowship Organized

Marston's leadership during this time helped move his church forward on many fronts. One deserves special attention.

The Board of Administration of the church in 1958 had adopted a statement that declared ". . . the proper objective of missionary endeavor is to develop the indigenous church as rapidly as possible wherever the Christian enterprise is planted." The board ". . . then took steps toward planning with national churches the organization of largely autonomous churches when national groups reach the stage of readiness for self-direction."

Bishop Marston wrote extensive notes on a month-long world trip he made in April 1960. He traveled with his friend, Dr. Byron S. Lamson, then General Missionary Secretary of the church. They visited the mission fields of the church in Egypt, India, Hong Kong, Taiwan, and Japan. The first Asia Area Fellowship Conference met in Japan, April 19-26 of that year. The Japanese planners arranged for the meetings in Osaka, Kobe, and Kyoto.

In 1961, Bishop Marston attended the first Southern Africa Fellowship Conference at Lundi Mission in Rhodesia (now Zimbabwe). On the same trip he organized the Ruanda-Urundi Annual Conference in central Africa—now divided into the two conferences of Rwanda and Burundi. (Growth has been phenomenal and Rwanda becomes a completely self-governing General Conference in 1985. Burundi is not far behind.)

From the experiences of these trips, Bishop Marston gained valuable insights into the overseas church. From his lengthy 1961 travel journal, these comments are especially appropriate:

> At a communion service, I received a new sense of the universal atonement as blacks knelt with whites. . . .
>
> Much autonomy is given the conferences, with a coordinated control by nationals and missionaries in partnership.
>
> Indeed it is time to place more responsibility on the national church. The days of missions may be numbered.
>
> Their [the nationals] ability in debate, their keen insight, their graciousness in it all, inspire confidence that they have inherent ability for self government. But their psychology is tribal and not democratic. There can be wide diversity in debate, but when the vote is taken, there is unanimity, usually in favor of the proposal. It is a strain on the missionaries to

witness democracy's struggle for birth.

In the beginning, the African church thought that it alone was Free Methodist. . . . But after attending the Africa Fellowship Conference, and now learning about the World Fellowship Conference, they realize that Free Methodism is a great church reaching around the world.

The World Fellowship Organizing Conference was held at Greenville, Illinois, in January 1962—during an ice storm which added even another new experience for many of the overseas delegates. Bishop Marston was elected the first president and served in that capacity until he retired.

Dr. Lamson told the story of the formation of the World Fellowship in his book, *To Catch the Tide,* (Winona Lake, Light and Life Press, 1963). He traced the trend of the far-sighted missionaries who believed the church in all areas of the world should have autonomy and freedom in developing their evangelistic ministries.

Concerning Bishop Marston's leadership overseas, Elmore Clyde (named to be General Missionary Secretary as of August 1, 1985), said, "His keen insights into the heart of the national, as well as his deep spiritual commitment, have served him well when conducting overseas annual conferences. Anyone who knew Bishop Marston knew him to be a parliamentarian par excellence; yet he was patient with and willing to learn from the national leaders. In the words of Bishop Marston, 'Our present task is not to establish and maintain missions so much as to extend missions and establish national churches.' Partly due to his vision we are seeing this happen around the world today."

Reflecting upon his 29-year term as bishop, Marston considered the establishment of our seminary training program and the emergence of a truly "world Free Methodist Church" as developments of major significance in which he had been instrumental.

Retirement Involvements

When the 1960 General Conference closed, Marston knew he had just four more years to serve as bishop. The General Conference had voted to set a younger retirement age, but the bishops then in office were exempted. Some thought that he would stand for reelection in 1964. He took the position that someone had to start the retirement process. He had two books in mind he wanted to write and thought it was time for him to step aside. He retired at the 1964 General Conference at the age of sixty-nine.

Two months after his retirement, Bishop Marston wrote in a letter dated August 22, 1964:

> I'll always have something to do and plenty, but I don't have to do it and that's the difference. We have relaxed and feel fit for years yet of emeritus existence. I do not find it difficult to keep from loading up with church problems for which others are now responsible. When I have a job resting on my shoulders, I am a nuisance. I'm relieved now that I can give the job a good letting alone.

However, the Church did give him a job to do. The 1964 General Conference established the Free Methodist Historical Committee, and Bishop Marston was named chairman. A center was to be opened for bringing together books, documents, photos, and any items relating to the heritage of the church. This gave him a challenge and actually a retirement career.

His study in connection with the writing of *From Age to Age a Living Witness* put him in a good position to gather material for the historical collection. He knew what was needed. He found much related to the history of Methodism in second-hand bookstores. Retired ministers and widows of ministers donated their libraries and collections of Free Methodist memorabilia. He advertised in denominational publications, sent out mailings, and with a library worker, catalogued a vast amount of material.

Housed in rooms at the Winona Lake, Indiana, headquarters of the Church, the collection now includes a 6,000 volume library, hundreds of pamphlets, documents and manuscripts, and complete sets of the Free Methodist *Yearbook* and *Book of Discipline;* and the periodicals—*The Earnest Christian, The Free Methodist,* and *Light and Life.* Scholars and researchers of many denominations, as well as Free Methodists, find the material useful.* In 1981, the Board of Administration officially named the center the Marston Memorial Historical Center.

---

*Frank Baker, Editor-in-Chief of *The Oxford Edition of Wesley's Works,* wrote, "You have a rich treasure of Wesley material in your collection. I have gone through your listings along with my annotated Union Catalogue. Quite a number of the items are rare, and you are way in front of many of the major libraries in this and other countries in having over seventy editions of Wesley's writings published during his own lifetime. Congratulations!"

Also assigned to the Historical Committee was the further development and maintenance of Centenary Memorial Park. This little park in Sanborn (formerly known as Pekin), New York, is on the site of the founding of the denomination. The park had been inaugurated by Light and Life Men International and was dedicated in 1960. Bishop Marston took extensive leadership following that time in improving the property and adding an exhibit pavilion with sixteen large panels showing in word and picture the heritage and mission of the Free Methodist Church.

Bishop Marston had looked forward to his retirement and found it fulfilling. However, at first he had problems, mainly relating to Social Security. His tender conscience caused him to scrutinize every law and talk often with the Social Security office to be sure he was obeying the complicated regulations that were then in effect. As a self-employed retiree, he was restricted in the number of hours he could work and the amount of additional income he could receive. This called for accurate record keeping and many limitations. It all added up to ulcers, resulting in another hospitalization.

Family Ties

During early retirement years the Marstons usually spent Christmas holidays in southern California at the Free Methodist parsonage of their daughter and husband, Evelyn and Jack Mottweiler, and children, Marston Hugo and Ann Lucile. Because of Grandpa's illness in early December, 1965, they could not make the trip that year. Instead, the Mottweiler family traveled to Greenville for the holidays—the last time in the Marston family home. Ann and Marston, even though they lived 2000 miles away from Grandma and "Gramps" Marston, felt a close relationship with Leslie and Lila Marston.

Robert (Bob) and Ardath (Mulholland) Marston lived in Michigan. Grandma and Grandpa could visit them often and enjoyed watching the growth and development of the grandchildren—two boys, Ronald Robert and Charles Ray, and twin girls, Julie Esther and Janet Lucile.

Tragedy struck the family in 1970 when Julie was killed by a truck while riding her bicycle in front of their home. The accident hit all the family hard. Bishop Marston described Bob as ". . . cut and bleeding deep down, but will come out of it—no doubt better able to minister to others." At the memorial service in his own church, Bob spoke from his heart to the overflow congregation, inviting them to know the Savior to whom Julie had gone.

The hurt did not heal quickly. Bob's father wrote to him in answer to questions such as "Where is Julie now?" He encouraged and advised Bob in his ministry. Gradually the sorrow changed to a mixture of loss and hope. They would see Julie again. They found encouragement in the words of King David, "I will go to him, but he will not return to me" (II Samuel 12:23).

The loss of a nine-year-old granddaughter hurt Bishop Marston and his wife Lila deeply. Their family was always given high priority in their affections. Countless phone calls, letters and cards, as well as visits back and forth, bonded them all together in a loving, caring relationship.

Robert and Ardath Marston and their family, three years before tragedy struck their home. Standing with parents is Ronald; seated are Charles, Julie, and Janet.

The Mottweiler family: Jack, Ann, Marston, and Evelyn.

Leslie and Lila Marston in a moment of
relaxation at home in Greenville, Illinois.

Bishops of the Free Methodist Church who served together for eleven years (1947 to 1958): C. V. Fairbairn, J. P. Taylor, L. R. Marston, and M. D. Ormston.

Bishop L. R. Marston at work on his monumental volume, *From Age to Age a Living Witness,* published by Light and Life Press in 1960 before the General Conference.

The birthplace of Free Methodism, now Centenary Memorial Park, Sanborn (formerly Pekin), New York, was dedicated in 1960. Bishop Marston speaking.

The World Fellowship organizing conference was held in Greenville, Illinois, in 1962. Delegates shown in picture are General Missionary Secretary Byron S. Lamson, Isaac Shembe (South Africa), Andres Brito (Dominican Republic), Victor Macy, missionary to Africa, and Bishop Marston, chairman.

The main work of his retirement years was Bishop
Marston's development of the Free Methodist Historical
Center. Many books and other items were collected
and catalogued for convenient reference.

These visitors to the Historical Center were given an
official tour by Bishop Marston during the 1974 General
Conference. Much interest was shown.

Honor Scroll

Awarded to <u>LESLIE RAY MARSTON, BISHOP EMERITUS</u>

by the <u>CENTRAL ILLINOIS</u>

ANNUAL CONFERENCE

in recognition of devoted service in the

MINISTRY of the FREE METHODIST CHURCH

as follows:

Bishop of the Free Methodist Church	29 Years
Dean, Professor, President of Greenville College	16 Years
(the last six years a Conference member)	
Member of General Conference	7 Times
Member General Board of Administration	29 Years
President, Board of Directors of F. M. Church	19 Years
President, World Fellowship of the F. M. Church	2 Years
Chairman of the Light & Life Hour Radio Com.	17 Years
Chairman of the Light & Life Press	19 Years

AUTHORSHIP: "Emotions of Young Children", "From Chaos to Character", "Youth Speaks", "From Age to Age a Living Witness".

Issued on <u>August 4</u> 19 <u>66</u>, at the annual session of the Conference at <u>Greenville, Illinois</u>.

Myron F. Boyd
PRESIDENT

Herbert H. Coates
SECRETARY

The Central Illinois Annual Conference, of which Bishop Marston was a member, presented this official Honor Scroll to him in August 1966, listing his achievements.

Bishop Emeritus L. R. Marston greeting World Fellowship delegates from overseas at the time of the 1974 General Conference in Winona Lake, Indiana.

At the General Conference of 1974, Bishop Marston read the Scripture lesson on Sunday morning.

L. R. Marston reporting for the Historical Committee at the 1969 General Conference.

15

"His Leaf Also Shall Not Wither"

Bishop Marston's roots were deep into the things of God, and he found good continuing involvement. In fact, he was too involved to actually get into the writing he had planned to do in his retirement. Significant among the writings he did do, however, is the paper he presented at the annual meeting of the Wesleyan Theological Society delineating his interpretation of the Wesleyan doctrine of entire sanctification.*

He worked vigorously on the founding and development of the Historical Center. He taught one or two courses in church history at Greenville College for several semesters. He worked with the leaders of the church who often sought his help for ongoing projects.

The passing of time made a difference. Advancing age necessitated change for Leslie and Lila who still made their home in Greenville, Illinois. The driving distance between Greenville and the Historical Center at Winona Lake (300 miles) seemed to be getting longer and longer.

Also, theirs was a close-knit family—Leslie and Lila's deep affections included their son's wife and daughter's husband.

So the idea of moving to Winona Lake began to grow. Their daughter Evelyn and husband Jack lived there, and son Bob and wife Ardath were only a few hours away in Jackson, Michigan. Because Leslie and Lila wanted and needed to be nearer to fam-

---

*Marston, L. R., "The Crisis-Process Issue in Wesleyan Thought," *The Wesleyan Theological Journal,* 1969. Used by permission. See Appendix V.

ily, the new retirement center, Grace Village, at Winona Lake, sounded interesting to them. Lila initiated an appointment with the administrator, and they were given brochures and prices. Leslie wanted to move in. Lila liked Grace Village but she couldn't face leaving Greenville. They had lived in Greenville for most of their married life—and each of them before that as students. Friends and family encouraged Lila, and finally in May of 1975, they made the move and were the first occupants of their attractive and comfortable apartment.

Earlier they had sold their house (built from Leslie's own blueprints after his election as bishop) and now their smaller retirement home (built from plans Leslie adapted). Lila found it a great trial to give up the neat little home across from the Greenville church. It helped some that they sold to their life-long friends, Dr. and Mrs. H. J. Long. Dr. Long had followed Leslie as Greenville's president.

At Grace Village, after the period of adjustment had passed, Lila liked the place and the people and proudly showed her guests around. She knew they had done the right thing.

*   *   *

Some of us could observe Bishop Marston close at hand in those days. He came regularly to the Historical Center. This was a delight to him, because in Greenville days he had had to do much work by correspondence and make frequent trips to Winona Lake.

He wrote some, but with difficulty. He told us of failing memory. "Really, it's not my memory," he would say with a grin. "It's my recall! I remember hundreds of things that happened fifty years ago, but I can't recall what I wrote a few pages back."

He still received speaking invitations but accepted few. What he did take he meticulously prepared for. Twenty years before he had dedicated a new church at Kalamazoo, Michigan. Now in October 1977, they wanted him to give the main message at their twentieth anniversary. He refused. They insisted. He finally agreed to offer the morning prayer. He spent much time in preparation for this assignment.

Dr. Richard Stephens asked the bishop to participate at his inauguration as president of Greenville College on October 29, 1978. Stephens wanted Marston to speak in connection with the naming of Archer Hall for a famous family, many of whom had graduated from Greenville. It would also give Marston recognition as a former president and a leader in education. He refused the invitation, but later with encouragement from his family and from Dr. Stephens, he agreed. He labored long over his short message on the Archers. He spoke about five minutes—his last public appearance.

Found among Bishop Marston's "jottings" were a statement entitled "About myself—written in my 80s," and a prayer written during private devotions at age 78:

> I consider myself an essentialist, but not a literalist. I am neither a profound thinker nor a clever phrase-maker. I do seek order and consistency in thought and action, and am inclined to seek origins and to trace trends, rather than to promote innovations. My respect for history restrains any revolutionary urge, and I agree with Sir Winston Churchill's claim that "The farther backward you can look, the farther forward you are likely to see."

> Heavenly Father, the cry of my heart this evening is that with approaching age my faculties may continue clear, my thinking lucid, my ministry in the pulpit one of ready speech and clarity, and mind open to truth, my heart responsive and sensitive to Thy Word, and to the opinions of others; may age be a period of ripening and not of decay, spiritually and intellectually. I pray, for thy glory, and in the name of Jesus Christ, my Lord and Saviour. Amen!

> (Later) At 84 years, I am still writing, declining in memory but in fair health—have much for which to be thankful.

Homegoing: "The Lord Knoweth the Way. . . ."

Just at Sunday school time on Father's Day morning, June 17, 1979, Evelyn received a call from her mother. Something was wrong with Daddy. He had difficulty walking and his speech was slurred.

Evelyn quickly cared for her class of preschoolers, then rushed to her parents' apartment. Her father's condition obviously demanded attention. Stopping by the church to pick up Jack, they took Bishop Marston to the emergency room of the local hospital. In spite of his pleas to let him have Father's Day dinner with his family first, they admitted him to the hospital. Father's Day was celebrated in the hospital room with two great-grandsons' pictures on the bedside table.

By evening, paralysis immobilized much of his right side. The next day Bob and Ardath arrived. Through the days ahead, he continued to worsen until the strokes left him nearly helpless and his speech almost unintelligible.

At one point physical and speech therapy were started, but there was little response. However, he maintained his sense of humor, responding with laughter when hospital visitors reminisced about such times as when he mistakenly took a sleeping pill instead of a vitamin tablet while holding an annual conference.

One of his last hospital visitors, Bishop W. Dale Cryderman, wrote, "His desire for worship was never diminished. Prayer with him was a worship experience, and on my last visit we worshiped together. I felt a strong squeeze from his good hand accenting my phrases of worship. Upon completion of the prayer, I heard from his lips a clear and resounding 'Amen!' "

The paralysis continued to spread. He eventually slipped into a coma. Release from this life came to the bishop on July 14, 1979, at 6:00 p.m., at the age of eighty-four years, seven months, and twenty-one days.

Memorial Service

The memorial service was held on July 17 in the Headquarters church. Bishop Donald N. Bastian, who had been Bishop Marston's pastor in Greenville, organized the service and presided. Bishop Paul N. Ellis, who had followed Dr. Marston as bishop, brought the message.

An educator, a colleague, a denominational leader, an evangelical churchman, and three bishops spoke words of high praise for Leslie R. Marston.* A tribute was also given by his son Robert.

Speaking for the Marston family, Bob talked with an openness that drew the listeners to him. His sincerity and his emotional control impressed us. As he told what his father meant to him from

---

*Appendix VI gives excerpts from the tributes and sermon.

childhood to manhood, the people got a new view of the great-ness of Bishop Marston.

Bob summarized his remarks with this statement:

> Across the years I found in Dad the fleshing out, the living out of total Christianity. In all extremes, in pressure situa-tions, and I had occasion to observe him in many of these, and in times of less stress, he has been my best example of the doctrine that he preached and practiced, entire sanctifi-cation. I needed a pattern for I was quick, as many folks are, to notice inconsistencies. But I saw in him the fruit of the Spirit because he possessed the filling of the Holy Spirit of God.

How did Leslie Marston succeed in a variety of leadership roles? Three words describe the reasons for his success.

Intelligence. His high intelligence served him well in both academic and work situations. He could cut through the insignifi-cant and come to the essential. He based his decisions on judg-ment, not on emotion or favoritism. And he made few mistakes.

Integrity. This word best describes Leslie Marston. While in the army he bought insurance to provide training for a substitute "if anything happens that I shouldn't be able to do anything in the world." He sent home "self-denial gifts for missions."

He refused to accept the psychological concensus of his student days that intelligence alone determined personality. He knew that his introverted temperament could cause him to not try to achieve. He could have accepted the current view and made something of it to his advantage. Integrity kept him from selfishly capitalizing on his own brilliance.

Leslie Marston strove to do his best in every position he held. He admired others who achieved. This led to especially high re-spect for men who succeeded financially. This did not discredit his integrity and none of us lost our respect for him. He was human, but the example of his life often put the rest of us to shame.

When he knew he had made a mistake he corrected it. A typical case involved a business meeting of General Conference to which he said, "Brethren, I believe that I was a little sharp yesterday and I want you to forgive me." Some of us who worked with him ex-perienced similar situations personally. His humility enhanced our love and appreciation for him.

Intensity. He worked hard on every project. In his remarks at the funeral Bob said, "Our home had an office that Dad used when he was there. He did a lot of his own correspondence. I have no idea how many millions of words Dad typed on that old manual Remington typewriter. But he did better with two fingers than most people do with ten."

Dr. Lloyd Knox (a pastor Bishop Marston picked to serve as publisher for the church) described him:

> In his visits to our parsonage, I recall the almost everlasting beat of the typewriter late at night, early in the morning. No task was approached, if he could help it, without careful, adequate preparation. Yet, he visited freely and long. He was an iron man. Later, I would express concern about one of his habits as he worked with characteristic energy . . . in his visits to Headquarters. He would work right through the lunch period, only stopping to visit the Coke and candy dispensers to secure his lunch.

Leslie Marston's intensity showed in his willingness to stay with a project or issue till he got results. His determination often carried the day.

In all his intensity, he did not lose his graciousness. He had an openness that made him approachable. Though his greatness might awe some people, he would quickly put them at ease. As a dinner guest or a house guest his commonness impressed his host families. They would marvel that such a man could make them feel so comfortable. He was gifted in winning the confidence of children, and they quickly responded to his warmth.

Leslie Ray Marston served with excellence as college professor and dean, child development director, college president, and bishop. He always left his place of service better than he found it. Surely Jesus must have welcomed him home with the greeting, "Well done, good and faithful servant!" (Matthew 25:21, NIV).

At Bishop Marston's memorial service, the congregation sang, "How Firm a Foundation." Nearly seven years earlier, Bishop Marston had penned the following note, later giving copies to Lila and Evelyn:

2:15 a.m., September 23, 1972

An hour or so ago I awakened, thinking it was near the rising hour. As I was lying on my bed, the lines of the old hymn, "How Firm a Foundation," came to mind in fragments. My heart was melted as the words echoed my testimony to God's hand on my life. Tomorrow I'll have lived on God's good earth seventy-eight years. I have no premonition of death's near approach, but when I have departed this life, be my remaining days few or many, let this hymn be sung by those who assemble to bid me farewell—until we meet again beyond the river!

—Leslie Marston

How firm a foundation, ye saints of the Lord,
   Is laid for your faith in his excellent Word!
What more can he say than to you he hath said,
   To you who for refuge to Jesus have fled?

"Fear not, I am with thee, O be not dismayed;
   For I am thy God, and will still give thee aid;
I'll strengthen thee, help thee and cause thee to stand,
   Upheld by my gracious omnipotent hand.

"When thro' the deep waters I call thee to go,
   The rivers of sorrow shall not overflow;
For I will be with thee thy trials to bless,
   And sanctify to thee thy deepest distress.

"E'en down to old age all my people shall prove
   My sov'reign, eternal, unchangeable love;
And when hoary hairs shall their temples adorn,
   Like lambs they shall still in my bosom be borne.

"The soul that on Jesus hath leaned for repose,
   I will not, I will not desert to his foes;
That soul, though all hell should endeavor to shake,
   I'll never, no, never, no, never forsake."

The dedication of Archer Hall at Greenville College on October 19, 1978, was the last public appearance of Bishop Emeritus Leslie Ray Marston.

Epilogue

Lila Marston lived on in their apartment at Grace Village, close to Evelyn and Jack and surrounded by friends and constant reminders of the fifty-eight years of marriage. On November 24, 1981, she went to join her Lord and her beloved Leslie.

Evelyn gave a tribute at the funeral of her mother, from which the following is excerpted:

> Many of the references in Proverbs chapter 31 apply so aptly to Mother. Looking well to the ways of her household had a more extensive meaning for her than for many women, because for twenty-nine years she was largely responsible for the running of the home, rearing the children, the training and discipline, and all of the daily decisions to be made in the home. This was, of course, because of Daddy's responsibilities which required that he be away from home often, and sometimes for long intervals. One of the things Bob and I remember most about those days was Mother's consistent conducting of family prayers and her regular attendance (with us in tow) at the services of the church. We have so much to thank her for now.
>
> Although there has been much joking about Dad's being a "child psychologist," he would be the first to agree (and I have heard him say it) that Mother deserves much of the credit for any success they may have had in child rearing!
>
> I mentioned Mother's strong emphasis in our home on prayer. This dependence on prayer was evident to the end. All through the years, whenever the family—or any part of it—would be together, she would always want us to pray before we separated. "Pray for me" was an often repeated request in her last few weeks. And how thankful we were to be there by her side to pray.

"Her children rise up, and call her blessed; her husband also, and he praiseth her. . . . a woman who feareth the Lord, she shall be praised."

—Proverbs 31:28, 30b

Lila and Leslie Marston celebrated their 56th wedding anniversary on August 16, 1977.

Appendices

Appendix I

The Marston experiments on the social characteristics of young children.

Otto Klineberg in *Social Psychology:*

> An ingenious study of introversion and extroversion in young children was made by L. R. Marston, the subjects ranging in age from 23 to 71 months, with an average of 51.3 months. The investigator manipulated an attractive toy, a teeter-totter, in the presence of the child. He ignored the child (unless the child approached him) for sixty seconds. Then he looked up at the child, but said nothing and did not smile. Thirty seconds later he looked up and smiled. Thirty seconds later he said, "Do you like the teeter-totter?" If there was no response, after thirty seconds he asked cordially, "Would you like to play with this teeter-totter?" If the child failed to approach, he said, "You may; come over and play with it." If the child still refused, the investigator urged him persistently. According to their reactions in this experiment, the children were classified into six degrees of introversion, ranging from the one extreme in which the child refused, unyieldingly, to play with the toy or fled from the room, to those at the extrovert end of the scale who did not wait for recognition, but promptly approached and played with the toy. The study is important because of the wide differences which it revealed in the children, and because it made use of an actual situation rather than a series of questions.

Experiments 2 through 5 further defined the behavior patterns of children:

The first experiment was used to measure the degree of social resistance. Experiment 2 measured the degree of compliance. It involved a toy duck and the promise to play a game with a lot of ducks if the child would open a box. The task wasn't easy, for the box was a portable typewriter case. Leslie watched and timed the child's efforts, then established a rating.

Experiment 3 continued the duck game. The typewriter case was full of small round boxes. The child was asked to choose between two boxes to get the one with the duck. This experiment measured the degree of caution.

Leslie designed experiment 4 to measure the degree of interest. He met the child at the entrance of the Mammal Hall of the University Museum. He gave the child the lead, letting him go anywhere he wanted. Leslie followed and recorded the trip on a plan of the hall. If the child refused to enter, Leslie led the way. In this situation he used a dotted line to show his path and a solid line for the child.

Experiment 5 used three mechanical toys to measure the degree of self-assertion. The child chose one of the three to play with. Leslie always gave the child a toy not chosen with the promise of the desired toy after he had played with the first one. Variations of this arrangement gave opportunity for self-assertion, which Leslie tabulated.

Leslie used children of parents of the University of Iowa Child Welfare Station for the experiments. He verified his findings with children in Des Moines and Cedar Rapids, Iowa. The results confirmed the validity of the original temperament rating scale he developed for the experiments.

Appendix II

Some of the major concepts of President Marston's inaugural address—"The Christian Ideal in Education." *(Greenville College Quarterly,* January 1929, Vol. 20, No. 4)

With scholarly skill he drew a line between the process of education and the product. He said, "The process is not an end in itself, but is rightly only a means to an end."

He then sketched various ways education had been used to achieve institutional purposes. The products became obedient subjects of the state, loyal adherents to a system of intellectual absolutism, and unquestioning followers of institutionalized religion.

Marston continued:

> I trust you have not been unduly wearied by the foregoing recital of answers to the central problem of education that runs throughout the history of organized society. Brief statements thereof are necessary to an appreciation of Christ's answer to the age-long conflict, to which we now turn our thought.
>
> That answer is best interpreted in the light of the influences of Christ's day which were mainly three: Greek, Roman, and Hebrew. As Joseph Kermon Hart has so clearly indicated in his thought-provoking book, *Democracy in Education,* these influences were all

highly institutionalized at the dawn of Christianity.

1. The Greek thinkers following Socrates had institutionalized thought, enmeshing the intellect in Platonic absolutisms and barren philosophical systems;
2. The Romans through their marvelous genius for organization and human engineering had perfectly institutionalized political and social relations, cramping the age with the absolutism of the practical;
3. The Jews had thoroughly institutionalized religion and morals, crushing the individual within the rigid limits of Pharisaical legalism.

These three forms of absolutism, intellectualism, practicalism, legalism, comprised a perfect machine without life or soul so that institutions were supreme and the individual man weighed naught. . . . Writing of this age the historian has said, "The race has lost its way; it has no way, no path ahead. It has come to the end, to absolute system, to completion of all its tasks, to certainty and hence to hopelessness.

Then Christ came!

Christ's message emphatically declared the love of a personal God, and the supreme worth of human personality. His message announced a kingdom, not of the external coming by observation, but a kingdom of God within. He heralded as the ideal not a crystallized absolute, not a static perfection of attainment, but living, dynamic growth. He taught not formalism but spirit and truth; not institutionalism, for the institution, He declared, was made for man, not man for the institution; not intellectualism, but conduct, for He said, "If any man will do the Father's will he shall know the doctrine;" not force, not authority, not compulsion, not legalism, but love, "Love your enemies," and "Love is the fulfilling of the law!" not an absolute world-ground nor far removed first cause without personal relationships with man, but a God who numbers the hairs of the head and whom man may address "Our Father;" not a message to a few, but the way by which "if any man enter in, he shall be saved. . . ."

Dr. Marston reviewed the educational aims of five outstanding thinkers of that day. He weighed each on the scale of reason and found it wanting. Then he gave the Christian answer.

It is our conviction that the only conception of life that possesses . . . satisfying completeness; that properly coordinates and integrates all of life's lesser aims and interests; . . . is the Christian ideal as taught by the founder of Christianity, a supreme love for God the Father, from which flows a universal love for man as brother.

Appendix III

Statement of Faith — National Association of Evangelicals

1. We believe the Bible to be the inspired, the only infallible, authoritative word of God.
2. We believe that there is one God, eternally existent in three persons, Father, Son, and Holy Ghost.
3. We believe in the deity of our Lord Jesus Christ, in His Virgin birth, in His sinless life, in His miracles, in His vicarious and atoning death through His shed blood, in His bodily resurrection, in His ascension to the right hand of the Father, and in His personal return in power and glory.
4. We believe that for the salvation of lost and sinful man regeneration by the Holy Spirit is absolutely essential.
5. We believe in the present ministry of the Holy Spirit by whose indwelling the Christian is enabled to live a godly life.
6. We believe in the resurrection of both the saved and the lost; they that are saved unto the resurrection of life, and they that are lost unto the resurrection of damnation.
7. We believe in the spiritual unity of believers in our Lord Jesus Christ.

Appendix IV

The Continental Divide in Christian Doctrine*

In the nature and being of God, which has preeminence? God's justice or His love? The answer to this question sets the direction of one's theology towards Calvinism or Arminianism.

The Calvinist, in his forensic system of thinking (as in a court procedure), makes much of the justice and the righteousness of God. In the light of God's absolute righteousness and justice, man is in corruption and wickedness, even under grace.

Because man has no righteousness and is incapable of good, his righteousness is imputed to him, as a credit secured for him through Christ's righteousness, and is not an imparted or implanted righteousness.

The man of sin remains in the heart and continues to battle with the new man in Christ until death brings deliverance. It is on the basis of this belief that, in extreme developments of Calvinism, some men have held

*Marston, L. R., *He Lived on Our Street,* Light and Life Press, 1979, page 139; also used in lecture form.

the belief that continuing in sin makes grace to abound.

By this, they mean that the Christian's violation of the law, that is, his sinning, glorifies God by revealing the inexhaustible store of God's grace through Christ's suffering for him on the Cross. Thus, the sinning believer says to God the Father, in effect, "Charge my sin to the account of your Son's inexhaustible deposit of grace made available to me through His death on the Cross."

The Apostle Paul writes of this in Romans 3:31, "Do we then make void the law through faith?" This is known in the history of doctrine as *antinomianism,* the word meaning "against law." Those holding this view maintain that the believer is made free from the law's requirement.

John Wesley encountered this doctrine more than two centuries ago. In his *Journal* under a 1746 date, he reported his conversation with a man who when Wesley asked him if he believed he had nothing to do with the law, replied, "I am not under the law: I live by faith." Then Wesley asked, "Have you, as living by faith, a right to everything in the world?" He answered, "I have; all is mine since Christ is mine." And he further asserted that this was true of the possessions of others — they were his, and even the bodies of consenting women. Wesley asked him if this was not sin, and his answer was, "Yes, to him that thinks it is a sin; but not to those whose hearts are free." In righteous indignation, Wesley exclaimed, in his *Journal,* against such perverters of the gospel, "Surely these are the firstborn children of Satan."

According to Calvinism, what is the nature of the atonement? It is in the nature of a court action, that is, forensic or legal. It is objectively accomplished the moment I confess Christ and believe on Him. I become a Christian by endorsing a contract, assenting to Christ's paying the price of my sins on Calvary. Thereby God's justice is satisfied for my sins—past, present, and future—and I can write checks at will on His infinite provisions of grace, and the Father will honor them! Christ is a cover for sin, not a cure.

According to this view, my righteousness is not actual, only positional. If I am in Christ, I am clothed with His righteousness. When God looks upon my sins through Christ's blood, He does not see my sins! The meaning of this view for ethics is readily apparent. In their emphasis on forensic or legal union with Christ, these extremists neglect ethical union with Christ, and they are likely to become careless in matters of Christian conduct.

If the justice of God overshadows His love, then man is ethically hopeless, and with a free conscience may sin daily in word, thought, and deed.

We are not to think that all Calvinists have carried to such excess the implications some have drawn from its underlying concepts anymore than have all Arminians accepted the way-out liberalism of some Arminians.

The tradition of Methodism, following John Wesley, is Arminianism warmed by Wesley's emphasis on an inner experience of grace which goes far deeper than the intellectual assent of Calvinism. Its pull is subjective in contrast with the Calvinist's objective emphasis. A fair comparison is brought out in the two views on the two doctrinal patterns regarding *total depravity*.

TOTAL DEPRAVITY

Calvinism's view holds that in man—apart from grace—there is naught but corruption and, as we have previously mentioned, maintains that the old man of sin continues an unceasing warfare until death releases the soul of the believer.

But the Arminian doctrine concerning *total depravity* holds that whereas in man, apart from grace, there is nothing by which, of himself by nature, he can merit God's favor and his soul's salvation, there are qualities in the natural man upon which grace can work. This milder view has led some to the humanistic position that there is a resident goodness in man's nature which can by nurture develop into Christian character.

Thus, moral ethics, which stress man's own righteousness, takes the place of atonement for sin among some Arminians, who idealize human nature and hold that eventually man's progress will bring the millennium of a perfect social order. But this dream of Arminian liberalism has been shattered by the moral corruption so evident today in the human condition the world around.

And some, nevertheless, have taken the further step to universalism, believing that someday, somehow, all mankind will be saved. Arminianism can, therefore, tend to let the love of God overshadow God's justice and righteousness.

We began our remarks with the question, Which has preeminence in the nature and essential being of God—His justice or His love? Have we arrived at an answer? If God is essentially neither justice nor love, what is He? If neither the logic of rigid Calvinism nor the subjectiveness of Arminianism is the answer, then where do we turn for an answer?

The answer is both God's justice and His love! We must balance on the continent's ridge—may we call it the Continental Divide in Christian doctrine? The justice of God and the love of God must be held in equipoise: love, the moving of God toward man and the motive of all His dealings with man; justice and righteousness, the regulating principle controlling even God's love in its expression.

"Let love be your guide" is a pernicious motto. Love is not a guide, not a controlling principle. *Love is a motive!* But motive needs direction, which means knowledge and discernment.

In the Cross are both God's love, moving Him toward man, and also His justice demanding satisfaction for sin. Loving man, God would save Him; but He cannot violate His own justice. The Cross satisfies that justice.

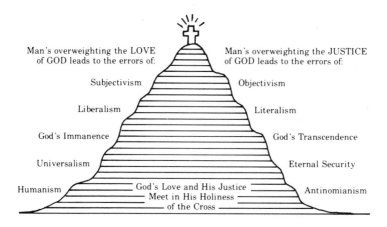

Man's overweighting the LOVE of GOD leads to the errors of:

Man's overweighting the JUSTICE of GOD leads to the errors of:

Subjectivism

Objectivism

Liberalism

Literalism

God's Immanence

God's Transcendence

Universalism

Eternal Security

Humanism

God's Love and His Justice
Meet in His Holiness
of the Cross

Antinomianism

THE CONTINENTAL DIVIDE IN CHRISTIAN DOCTRINE

As Christians move nearer the Cross of Jesus Christ in which are displayed in perfect harmony both God's Justice and His Love, they move nearer one another, and their differences diminish. The equipoise of *love* and *justice* in God's dealings with mankind leans neither toward the cold, legal atonement of historic Calvinism and its extreme of Antinomianism on the right, nor toward Arminianism's drift to liberal humanism and its extreme of Universalism on the left. God's transcendence and His immanence are a balanced synthesis.

Appendix V

The Crisis-Process Issue in Wesleyan Thought*

1. Introduction

In the definition of Christian holiness the crisis-process problem has become a subject of keen discussion in Wesleyan ranks today, even as a century ago it had become an issue in historic Methodism.

The scope of this paper is threefold. First, to sketch the background of the problem set by John Wesley's persisting devotion to the term "Christian perfection" as essentially synonymous with the term "entire sanctification" to designate a second crisis in Christian experience. Second, to present a point of view which differentiates the two terms by identifying "Christian perfection" with the continuing process of spiritual growth from the new birth to life's end, and conceives of "entire sanctification" as a

*Marston, L. R., *Wesleyan Theological Journal,* Vol. 4 No. 1, spring 1969. Also printed in three installments, *The Free Methodist,* May-June 1969. Used by permission.

normal event of heart-cleansing and love-infilling occurring within the lifetime process. Finally, to develop this approach by reviewing the writings of a leader in the holiness movement of a century ago whose position, strangely enough, has been obscured if not lost to the present century.

II. John Wesley and the Mystics

In John Wesley's prolonged quest for holiness as the ground upon which, in his thinking, he must claim justification in God's sight, he became enamored with the Christian mystics and their pursuit of perfection. Some of these mystics were what Albert C. Outler (1) has called *voluntaristic* and others *quietistic*. By the former we understand Outler to mean activists who take Jesus Christ as their pattern, and strive by a strenuous legalism to achieve a perfection in accord therewith.

The *quietists,* on the other hand, were subjectivists who sought inward union with Jesus Christ by way of prayer, passive contemplation, and detachment from the world because of its inherent corruption. By demeaning the human body as inherently evil and removed from the spirit by an impassable gulf, some quietists drifted into crass antinomianism on the assumption that vile deeds of the body could not possibly come into contact with, and thereby contaminate, one's spiritual being.

In his questing years, the spiritual emphasis of the quietists appealed to Wesley, but he drew back from their influence when he observed the antinomian trend of their teachings. But this was not until the choking grip of subjectivism had brought him very near the brink of tragedy. While on his Georgia mission he analyzed the hazards of the quietistic mystics in a letter to his brother, Samuel, Jr., in which he made this confession: "I think the rock on which I had nearest made shipwreck of faith was the writings of the mystics: under which I comprehend, and only those, who slight any of the means of grace." (2)

He had followed also the path of activism by most dutifully performing good works. Upon his return from America, however, he came under the influence of the learned and pious Peter Böhler, and by him was convinced of the futiliy of works-righteousness. About a fortnight prior to his Aldersgate deliverance, Wesley wrote a sharp rebuke to his former counselor, William Law, charging him with teaching obedience to the law and Jesus Christ as the pattern of the law's fulfillment, but failing to point him to simple faith in Jesus Christ as Saviour. (3) By this time Wesley had accepted intellectually Peter Böhler's tutelage in salvation by faith, but he had not yet grasped its full meaning in the assurance of personal salvation.

III. John Wesley Discovers the Way of Faith

A few days later this assurance did come to him, and although for several months thereafter he was beset by severe inner struggles, he did not again sink into the morass of his former miseries of mysticism. When, because of these struggles, for a time he so completely lost his assurance of salvation that he asserted that no longer was he a Christian, nevertheless he stoutly affirmed the validity of the experience of divine forgiveness he had received at Aldersgate.

Some call the later Wesley a mystic on the basis of his Aldersgate conversion and his emphasis thereafter on a heart religion. The scope of this paper does not permit extended discussion of this claim, but we venture to offer a few observations. The later course of Wesley's active and fruitful life reflects an inner organization by which he far transcended his earlier mysticism. Outler writes of his mature view of perfection as calling for "holiness in the world . . . active holiness in this life." (4) He who had sought the reality of God earnestly but in vain by mystical routes, both voluntaristic and quietistic, entered at Aldersgate into a personal relationship with God through faith in Jesus Christ as his Saviour.

His early failures and this later discovery of the way of faith point up the difference between "mystical religion" and "personal salvation"—a distinction his spiritual descendants should hold clearly in focus while facing the dazzling blur of the world's present religious confusion. Mysticism is the quest for reality by way of man's own capacities, whether subjectively or objectively exercised. Evident to all is the legalism of the voluntaristic mystic, and Wesley came to discern also that even his quietism had been a form of self-salvation. But true faith is the response, not of a special mystical faculty or of any power of one's being, but of one's essential self—his entire being—to the call of God.

IV. Wesley's Persisting Emphasis on Christian Perfection

Now we return to pre-Aldersgate Wesley and the writers who so largely influenced him in his early adult years. In *A Plain Account of Christian Perfection* (5) Wesley has outlined the steps of his approach to the doctrine of Christian perfection over a period of more than forty years, beginning with the year of his graduation from Oxford University and his ordination as deacon in 1725.

According to his retrospect, in 1725 Wesley read Bishop Taylor's *Rules of Holy Living and Holy Dying.* This led him to dedicate his entire life to God—his thoughts, words, actions—so deeply did the book impress him with the importance of purity of intention. In 1726 he read *The Christian Pattern* by a Kempis, from which he understood that "simplicity of intention, and purity of affection" are " 'wings of the soul' without which she can never ascend to the mount of God"—here indeed is language of the mystic!

A year or two later he read William Law's two classics of devotion,

Christian Perfection and *Serious Call.* These led him "to be all devoted to God—to give Him," he said, "all my soul, my body, my substance." And then in 1729, Wesley reports, he became "a man of one book." He resorted to the Bible "as the one, the only standard of truth, and the only model of true religion." Thereby he was brought to see religion "as a uniform following of Christ, an entire inward and outward conformity to our Master." On January 1, 1733 he reports a sermon which he preached in St. Mary's, Oxford, on the subject "The Circumcision of the Heart." In that sermon he defined a "circumcised heart" in terms of cleansing, holiness, and becoming "perfect even as the Father in heaven is perfect." This was more than five years before his Aldersgate conversion!

And Wesley extends the record, adducing still other instances to attest his having advocated Christian perfection long before the publication of *A Plain Account* in 1765. But these instances, and those recounted above more specifically, point alike to the conclusion that to John Wesley, and to his favorite authors with a leaning toward mysticism, Christian perfection signified, not so much a state of grace initiated by a spiritual crisis subsequent to the new birth, as a lifetime striving to reach the Christian ideal by following Jesus as pattern. These earlier teachings and searchings did indeed hold to the scriptural standard of holiness of heart and life, but Wesley seems not so specific on a second crisis during the period covered by his retrospect as he had become at the time he wrote *A Plain Account.*

V. Crisis-Process: Toward a Solution

Can it be that there is a valid concept of Christian perfection applicable to any and every stage and phase of the Christian life, both before and following the crisis of entire cleansing? In the course of Wesley's evangelistic endeavors following Aldersgate, he observed that a second crisis occurred in the experience of many believers some time after their conversion crisis. We ask, did Wesley incorrectly identify this second crisis with the initiation of the Christian perfection he long had advocated? Should he not have related this second crisis to that perfection by defining it as the consummation of the process of sanctification which, he had consistently taught, begins in regeneration? Has the confused thinking concerning crisis and process developed in measure from Wesley's equating Christian perfection with entire sanctification, whereas the former may be a lifelong perfecting process and the latter an event of the moment, experientially realized and belonging within the context of that perfecting process?

A century after Wesley an affirmative answer to such questions was offered by one now little remembered within American Methodism.

VI. Benjamin T. Roberts

As a young man Benjamin T. Roberts had chosen the law as his profession, but when nearing his bar examination he was converted and then began his preparation for the Methodist ministry. Thus it happened that in Wesleyan University Roberts became a classmate of Daniel Steele with whom he shared academic honors and, from Wesleyan, he received the degrees Bachelor of Arts and Master of Arts, and was elected to Phi Beta Kappa. His career following his university training combined the Christian ministry, church administration, and religious journalism.

From 1860 to his death in 1893 Roberts edited and published *The Earnest Christian,* an independent family magazine similar in character but, some would say, journalistically superior to the more widely known *Guide to Holiness.* In his *Story of Methodism,* A. B. Hyde said of Roberts, "He was a brilliant and effective speaker, and a concise, clear, energetic writer." (6) A contributor to such a standard work as McClintock and Strong's *Cyclopedia of Biblical, Theological and Ecclesiastical Literature* characterized Roberts as "a writer of considerable power" whose "editorials, tracts, and essays display argumentative ability, and the faculty of uttering truth concisely." (7)

This brief of Roberts' career and accomplishments has been presented to establish his competence in the religious and literary fields. We forego discussion of his far-seeing concern with social, economic and ecclesiastical reforms as not relevant to the purpose of this paper.

VII. The Holiness Teachings of Roberts

Following the death of B. T. Roberts in 1893, his son, Benson H. Roberts, compiled from his father's editorial writings, which had extended across the third of a century, a book of 256 pages under the title, *Holiness Teachings.* (8) Timothy L. Smith, well-known scholar within Wesleyan ranks today, has characterized this book as emphasizing "the ideal of perfect character toward which he (Roberts) believed perfect love and all other authentic religious experiences tend." (9) We list herein six emphases of *Holiness Teachings,* five of which are stated without amplification. The sixth, because of its direct bearing on the crisis-process issue, is considered here more in detail.

(1) *Initial sanctification.* Sanctification begins with the new birth by which the sinner becomes "in an important sense, a holy man," with power over his impulses to sin.

(2) *Entire sanctification.* In entire sanctification, full cleansing comes with a man's complete surrender of every power and possession to the Holy Spirit's control, such that all his motives become promptings of perfect love to God and to all men.

(3) *The human element.* Entire sanctification renders a man not one whit less human, depriving him of no trait or power with which he is constitutionally endowed by creation.

(4) *Backsliding.* If the vital connection of faith for cleansing is broken,

the holiness of the sanctified yields to the invasion of corrupting tendencies to sin, and these propensities may lead again to the outward transgressions of a backslidden state.

(5) *Perfect love.* The vital core of entire sanctification is perfect love expressed to God and man through all one's powers of soul, strength and mind, however widely these powers may vary in degree and in rate of progress with different persons.

As thus briefly stated, these emphases may seem commonplace. But supported in the book itself by Roberts' pungent phrasing of his clear insights and by his lucid applications and scriptural citations, they offer a clear guide to holiness. Moreover, they provide a framework in which Roberts' distinctive contribution to the crisis-process issue may be viewed.

VIII. Christian Perfection

In the term "Christian perfection" we reach the point at which Roberts diverged from the traditional Wesleyan usage to give a broader meaning thereto than that included in either "entire sanctification" or "perfect love." Roberts applied the term to the entire span of a sincere Christian's development toward full maturity. It was his claim that the biblical command to be perfect refers, not to any specific step or crisis in the Christian life, but to its every phase and stage. He wrote:

> The command "be perfect" does not express any well known, definite act like the command "repent"; nor any particular experience like being "born again." It is taken in a wider sense; with a greater latitude of meaning. It applies to a child of God in various stages of his experience. A blade of corn may be said to be perfect in a dozen different stages of its growth. But if, before it is ripe, it stopped growing, it would not be perfect. So, at a certain period of his experience, a person may be said to be a perfect Christian, and yet his attainments in piety be small in comparison with what they are after fifty years of toil and sorrow. (10)

Roberts illustrated this point further by drawing upon the increasing perfection of the intellectual powers, which at one stage may be perfect but later reach higher perfections with further growth and discipline.

> A young man leaves the district school for the academy. He has studied hard and begins to reap some of its fruits. The teacher, proud of his pupil, says: "He is perfect in his mathematics. He can solve every problem in the hardest arithmetic." After three years in the academy with a mathematics lesson every day, he is sent to college, recommended as "perfect in mathematics." He is well versed in algebra, geometry and trigonometry. After studying mathematics in college four years, having completed his course, he

graduates with the highest honors of the mathematical department. He then goes to some special school and spends perhaps three more years in studying mathematics as applied to astronomy or to civil engineering. Then again he is pronounced perfect in his well-mastered study. At the end of a life of unremitting study, we hear him say with the immortal Sir Isaac Newton, "I seem like a child standing upon the shore of the ocean gathering pebbles. I have picked up here and there a pearl, while the great ocean of truth lies unexplored before me."

So when one becomes a Christian his conversion may be perfect; when his heart is purified by faith he may be perfectly sanctified; and still after years of growth in grace we hear him saying with Job when he got sight of God, "Wherefore I abhor myself and repent in dust and ashes." Yet God had twice pronounced him perfect. (11)

Thus Roberts maintained that Christian perfection is not a definite step to be taken by faith, as regeneration or entire sanctification, but is a continuous process and inclusive category involving day by day obedience and discipline, and warns that "we must not confound the perfection which the Gospel requires with perfect love or entire sanctification. The Scriptures do not use these terms as synonymous." And he cites passages:

We never read in the Bible of any being made perfect by faith. We read of persons being "justified by faith" (Rom. 5:1; 9:30; Gal. 3:24), of being "sanctified by faith" (Acts 15:9; 26:18), but never once of a person being made perfect by faith. Quite another element enters into the making of the saints perfect.

"For it became him, for whom are all things, and by whom are all things, in bringing many sons unto glory, to make the captain of their salvation perfect through sufferings" (Heb. 2:10). The perfection which the Gospel enjoins upon the saints can only be attained by fidelity in doing and patience in suffering all the will of God. A symmetrical, well-balanced, unswerving Christian character is not obtainable at once. (13)

If Roberts here rightly divides the Word of truth, the final perfection of the Christian is not an instantaneous gift of God's grace to be received alone by the prayer of faith, but comes in the lifelong processes of a ripening Christian character. "We are to seek it," says Roberts, "as a well disposed boy seeks a vigorous manhood by shunning the vices and overcoming the temptations to which he is exposed, and by doing faithfully the duties to which he is called." (14)

Conceived thus, Christian perfection is not static, given once for all as a state of grace in which the Christian may rest. It is a conquest leading to further conquests by faithful service and patient endurance.

IX. Wesley and Roberts

Nowhere in his *Holiness Teachings* did Roberts refer to Wesley's "second-crisis" concept of Christian perfection as differing from his own "life-process" concept. Perhaps he discerned in Wesley's writings a hint of the insights that had come so clearly to him. Certainly his intent was not critical opposition to Wesley's concept, for then he must have made a direct attack. His purpose could have been to clarify a cloudy spot in Wesley's analysis of Christian experience.

In his later maturity Wesley wrote what strongly inclines towards Roberts' position. In one of his letters he states that there are two ways "wherein it pleases God to lead his children to perfection: doing and suffering." Also worthy of note as pointing to Wesley's vague anticipation of Roberts' life-process concept are these words concerning Christian perfection in *A Plain Account:* "It is improvable. It is so far from lying in an indivisible point, from being incapable of increase, that one perfected in love may grow in grace far swifter than he did before." (15)

John L. Peters has observed that in such a statement, "Wesley implies a distinction which he generally fails to maintain . . . between entire sanctification as an event and Christian perfection as a continuing process of which that event is a part." It would be difficult indeed to formulate a more adequate statement of Roberts' distinction between entire sanctification and Christian perfection than this phrasing by Peters. Peters further asserts of Wesley's statement that here, "Wesley displays one of the most significant, *and neglected,* facets of his teaching." (16)

Regarding entire sanctification Wesley and Roberts were in agreement. Neither held to a doctrine of "gradualism" which repudiates a crisis in the entire cleansing of the heart and its infilling with love, and each maintained that the sanctification initiated in regeneration is consummated in cleanness—a completed act, as signified by the aorist tense of the verb "cleanse" (katharisomen) in II Corinthians 7:1, ". . . let us cleanse ourselves from all filthiness of the flesh and spirit, perfecting holiness in the fear of God" (KJV).

Furthermore, both Wesley and Roberts held that beyond the event of heart-cleansing and its correlated infilling of love, there is in the normal course of Christian experience a continuous progress in holiness as signified by *"perfecting" (epitelountes)* in the passage above cited. This love, although perfect in quality, is capable of increase in degree and in scope of application to ever-widening areas of life's relationships, even as Peter admonished Christians to "grow in grace and in a knowledge of our Lord and Saviour Jesus Christ" (II Peter 3:18, KJV).

But as already noted, Roberts explicitly set forth in *Holiness Teachings* what seems contrary to the general tenor of Wesley's position, in holding that spiritual progress of the sincere Christian prior to the second crisis of entire sanctification may properly be ascribed in progress in Christian perfection. Wesley applied the term Christian perfection only to such progress as follows the post-conversion crisis of entire cleansing.

X. By Way of Conclusion

Near the close of *A Plain Account of Christian Perfection* Wesley wrote:

> I say again, let this perfection appear in its own shape, and who will fight against it? It must be disguised before it can be opposed. It must be covered with a bearskin first, or even the wild beasts of the people will scarce be induced to worry it. (17)

Hopeful as Wesley may have been that *A Plain Account* would tear off the bearskin and correctly disclose the distinctive teachings of Methodism, it seems that a corner of the bearskin still covered at least one area. Further unveiling was left to one of Wesley's devoted followers of the succeeding century. In the light of this unveiling as described in the preceding pages, and at the risk of incurring the charge of presumption, we conclude with two observations:

(1) Much of the centuries-long confusion and controversy following upon Wesley's choice of the term "Christian perfection" might have been avoided had he not identified this favorite concept of his questing years with the second-crisis experience of early Methodists, and if instead he had applied the term to the normal progress of the obedient and fully trusting Christian, from the new birth through every stage to the ultimate perfection of eternity.

(2) The somewhat stultifying figure of "states of grace" (should we say "plateaus"?), lamented by Wesley himself, might then have yielded place to the figure of an ascent — continuous upward progress in the spiritual life of the Christian, in which occurs the crisis-event of entire sanctification, and following which, in consequence of the Christian's deliverance from the drag of inbred sin, the angle of ascent more nearly approaches the vertical—that ultimate perfection of eternity (see Heb. 6:1; 12:22-24).

(continued on following two pages)

DIAGRAM REPRESENTING "PLATEAU" VERSUS "DYNAMIC" CONCEPTS OF CHRISTIAN EXPERIENCE

The charts we now present place in contrast "plateau" and "dynamic" concepts of Christian experience and growth. "A" represents the former concept, and properly emphasizes the fact of crisis in spiritual experience but neglects intervening progress—a hazard of the designation "state of grace" admitted by Wesley. "B" exhibits the dynamic concept of growth while maintaining the pivotal points of crisis, thus combining crisis and process.

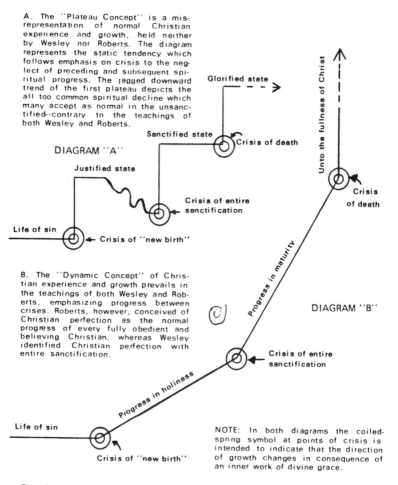

A. The "Plateau Concept" is a misrepresentation of normal Christian experience and growth, held neither by Wesley nor Roberts. The diagram represents the static tendency which follows emphasis on crisis to the neglect of preceding and subsequent spiritual progress. The jagged downward trend of the first plateau depicts the all too common spiritual decline which many accept as normal in the unsanctified—contrary to the teachings of both Wesley and Roberts.

DIAGRAM "A"

Glorified state

Sanctified state · Crisis of death

Justified state

Crisis of entire sanctification

Life of sin · Crisis of "new birth"

Unto the fullness of Christ

Crisis of death

Progress in maturity

B. The "Dynamic Concept" of Christian experience and growth prevails in the teachings of both Wesley and Roberts, emphasizing progress between crises. Roberts, however, conceived of Christian perfection as the normal progress of every fully obedient and believing Christian, whereas Wesley identified Christian perfection with entire sanctification.

DIAGRAM "B"

Crisis of entire sanctification

Progress in holiness

Life of sin

Crisis of "new birth"

NOTE: In both diagrams the coiled-spring symbol at points of crisis is intended to indicate that the direction of growth changes in consequence of an inner work of divine grace.

The above charts accompany, and are a part of "The Crisis-Process issue in Wesleyan Thought," a paper presented before the Wesleyan Theological Society at Olivet Nazarene College, Nov. 2, 1968, by Leslie R. Marston.

DOCUMENTATION

(1) Albert C. Outler, Ed. *John Wesley* (New York: Oxford University Press, 1964), p. 252.

(2) John Telford, Ed. *The Letters of John Wesley* (London: Epworth Press, 1931), I, p. 207.

(3) Nehemiah Curnock, Ed. *The Journal of the Rev. John Wesley, A.M.* (London: Epworth Press, 1938), VIII, 319, *et. seq.*

(4) Outler, *op. cit.*

(5) John Wesley, *A Plain Account of Christian Perfection* (London: Epworth Press, 1952), p. 5, *et seq.*

(6) A.B. Hyde, *The Story of Methodism* (New York: M.W. Hazen Co., 1888), p. 319.

(7) N.S. Gould "Free Methodists" in *Cyclopedia of Biblical, Theological and Ecclesiastical Literature* (New York: Harper & Brothers, 1876), pp. 187—189.

(8) Benson H. Roberts, Compiler-Editor, *Holiness Teachings Compiled from the Editorial Writings of the late Rev. Benjamin T. Roberts, A.M.* (N. Chili, N.Y.: Earnest Christian Publishing House, 1893), 256 pp.

(9) Timothy L. Smith, *Revivalism and Social Reform* (New York-Nashville: Abingdon Press, 1957), p. 131.

(10) Benson H. Roberts, *op. cit.* p. 209, *et seq.*

(11) *Ibid.,* 210, *et seq.*

(12) *Ibid.,* p. 212, *et seq.*

(13) *Ibid.,* p. 211.

(14) *Ibid.,* p. 212.

(15) *John Wesley, op. cit.* p. 8.

(16) John L. Peters, *Christian Perfection and American Methodism* (New York-Nashville: Abingdon Press, 1956), p. 52.

(17) John Wesley, *op. cit.,* p. 110.

Appendix VI

Excerpts from tributes to Bishop Emeritus Leslie R. Marston at his funeral on July 17, 1979.

Byron Lamson:

. . . He was a giant in mind, heart, and hand. His performance in every area—as college professor and president, and his long and distinguished career as bishop—was a model to be admired and emulated. He always seemed to be a standard.

He was my friend and critic. We were members of the same boards. Honest views and attitudes frequently put us in opposite camps, but we loved each other the more.

His recent letter to me said, "Let's plan to be on the same street up there. I want to be near you." . . . By the grace of God, we will see you in the morning on that "street up there."

W. Richard Stephens:

It was at Greenville College that Dr. Marston spent the major part of his career in the professional role for which he was trained—teaching. It was there that he taught hundreds of students how they could love Jesus Christ with their minds, and as I travel to alumni meetings across this land, always and ever someone says: "When I was there, Dr. Marston taught me this way, or he said that, and he impressed me and left an imprint for good on my life." These people literally rise up today and call him blessed.

He was a man far too large for our small town and for our school, and his influence spread far and wide. He rubbed arms with giants of thought in the modern world. I have studied books and sources during that period of time and have been shocked, surprised, and glad with joy for there would appear an article by Leslie Ray, along with the giants of that day. He lived his faith in front of those men.

Lloyd Knox:

In Bishop Marston there was strength, order, and direction. His leadership was always marked by intelligence, rationality, and immense energy. Yet, underneath there flowed deep, reverent, and tender feelings.

As chairman of the Administrative Commission, he always operated a tight ship. He had an appreciation for well prepared reports and well-researched, adequately defended proposals. . . . He respected intelligent argument, reasoned philosophy, and innovative proposals. He wanted no "yes" man on his team. I should know, for I expect I adequately tested him at this point. And still there came to be a bond between us filled with warmth. . . . He was indeed a multidimensional man, and therefore had a multidimensional impact on his church and the evangelical community.

Bishop Paul N. Ellis (funeral sermon):

. . . Most of us know that in the total view of life, the Christian witnesses his faith and his triumph in Christ much more by what he is than by what he says. . . . Leslie Marston has left us this kind of a testimony, written large to a steadfast faith in Christ that made him triumphant to the very end. He exemplified what it means to really live out the Christian life when Christ is at the very center of our living. . . .

When the church called, he always responded. He somehow believed that the call of the church was the call of God upon his life. . . . He believed that the church knew the mind of God. . . . As bishop, he became the pastor to hundreds of pastors and their families and the people of God throughout the entire denomination.

In his personal life and family life, Bishop Marston exemplified the plus of Christian living. Christ was at the very center of his home. He fulfilled the requirements of the Word of God that a bishop be the husband of one wife and rule his household well. And the result has been that the children of that home are distinguished Christian servants as you have come to know.

Our dear friend Bishop Marston would be very reticent to point to himself in any way, but I feel, like Paul, that he would have the right to say to us today, "Follow me, as I follow Christ." . . . I would urge you today, let us determine to follow to the end.

Leslie and Lila Marston